Times and Seasons II

Times and Seasons II

Homilies for Church Year B

SERGIO P. NEGRO

Edited by Sharon M. Young

WORDWORKS
Fresno, California

Text © 1999 by the Most Rev. John T. Steinbock,
Bishop of the Diocese of Fresno, California

Illustrations © 1999 by Donna Castelazo Locati

Cover: "The Star People"

Library of Congress
Catalog Card Number: 99-76117

ISBN: 0-9641404-6-2

This book was set electronically in Adobe Caslon type.
Paper is Georgia Pacific Proterra, an acid-free, 60 percent
recycled stock. Printed by Jostens, Visalia, California.

Published by WORDWORKS
An imprint of :
Sixth Street Press
3943 N. Sixth Street
Fresno, California 93726

Contents

Foreword

The Second Vatican Council in its *Dogmatic Constitution on Divine Revelation* states:

> All clerics, particularly priests of Christ who . . . are officially engaged in the ministry of the Word, should immerse themselves in the Scriptures by constant sacred reading and diligent study. For it must not happen that anyone becomes 'an empty preacher of the Word of God to others, not being a hearer of the Word in his own heart . . . .'

Fr. Sergio Negro was raised and ordained in the years preceding Vatican II, but it is evident from his homilies that he took these words of the Council to heart both in the priority he gave to his personal study and in his willingness to be shaped by the sacred Scriptures. As a result, his preaching demonstrated a unique insight into God's Word.

Even more important for his priestly ministry, Fr. Negro had a remarkable ability to convey his understanding of Scripture through a homiletic style that both inspired and challenged his listeners for nearly forty-six years of priestly service. Even after retiring from parish ministry to assume responsibilities as Vicar General of the Diocese, Fr. Negro continued to put quality time into his homily preparation.

I thank those who have prepared this selection of Fr. Negro's homilies, published for our personal reading and reflection. May his words continue to find a place in our hearts and challenge us to put God's Word into action in our lives.

✝ Most Rev. John T. Steinbock
Bishop of the Diocese of Fresno

Sergio P. Negro
March 30, 1929 - April 18, 1999

Preface

In the seventy years of his life, Father Sergio Negro made a difference in the lives of the people he met—members of his parishes, students he taught at the university, his fellow priests, and citizens of the larger community. A *Fresno Bee* editorial following his death was titled: "The death of a respected cleric saddens an entire community." The editor stated: "The death Sunday of the Rev. Sergio P. Negro was a blow to the Fresno diocese he served as vicar general and to the Fresno St. Paul Newman Center, which he helped found. It was also a loss keenly felt far beyond the boundaries of the local Catholic community."

A few weeks after Father Negro's death, the *Bee* carried an essay by a former colleague and long-time friend offering the perspective of a non-believer. Jim Dunn-Smith, professor emeritus of philosophy at California State University, Fresno, and a self-proclaimed atheist, described his friendship with Father Negro, stating in part: "It was the strength of [his] faith that made it possible for him to accept, even to seek out other convictions, other faiths, even the rejection of faith, not as foils for his arguments or as possible conversions but as sources of enlightenment. This faithful openness made our friendship possible."

Born in Pinerolo, Italy, in 1929, Sergio Negro came to the United States in 1948 and earned his bachelor of arts in philosophy from St. John's Seminary in Camarillo, California. He received a master of arts in education from California State University, Fresno, and a doctorate in theology from Graduate Theological Union in Berkeley, California.

He was ordained a priest in 1953, and served the Diocese of Fresno at St. John's Cathedral and the Shrine of St. Therese before beginning his thirty-year ministry at St. Paul Newman

Center. When he left Newman Center in 1994, he served the diocese as Vicar General and continued the work he had begun in 1990 as ethics consultant at Fresno's Saint Agnes Medical Center. He died on April 18, 1999, a few weeks after his seventieth birthday.

Father Negro's homilies brought inspiration, challenge, and comfort to thousands of parishioners during his ministry. Through his first book, *Times and Seasons,* published in 1994, his powerful preaching reached an even larger audience. *Times and Seasons* was a collection of homilies from all three cycles of the liturgical year, published to honor Father Negro at the conclusion of his Newman Center ministry. His final homily from that period is included in this volume. Through this second volume of homilies, and in the two volumes to follow, Father Negro's vibrant faith will continue to touch the hearts and lives of both believers and seekers for many years to come.

In the introduction to *Times and Seasons,* Father Negro wrote about his faith and his approach to preaching:

> I believe that the God of Abraham, Isaac, and Jacob, and the God of Jesus of Nazareth, has revealed himself in historical events and historical persons, and that these encounters with the living God—experienced, remembered, told, and retold in faith—have been passed on to us for countless generations through the written word and the living faith of the church community and of every faith-filled and grace-filled person who has read or heard the Word of God.
>
> Preaching has never been easy for me, and neither the preparation nor the presentation of the Sunday homily seems to have become easier over the years. If anything, they have become more difficult. It was simpler to hunt for the verse that said what I wanted to say, much simpler than to listen to the Scripture texts with mind and heart open to the encounter with the God who is willing to lift the veil of his mystery ever so slightly, so that we can be touched by the depth of his infinity and the immediacy of his love.

We have organized this volume of homilies for cycle B according to the Sundays and feast days of the year 1999–2000. The unusually late date of Easter in 2000 necessitated some minor adjustments.

Thanks to Bishop John T. Steinbock, Fr. Perry Kavookjian, Donna Locati, Dr. Jose and Shirley Canales, Dr. Thomas and Mary Kay Buckley Hackett, Barbara and Gary Marsella, and Jane and Paul Worsley for their support. At Father Negro's request, all proceeds from the sale of the first volume of *Times and Seasons* went to support charitable work in the Fresno community. Following the publication and sale of Volume IV, all profits will be similarly disbursed.

We invite you to nourish your mind, heart, and spirit with Father Negro's words. Surely here was a man of God, a man for all times and seasons, a man who lived the faith he proclaimed. As he stated at the conclusion of his homily for Epiphany 1988, which begins on page 23:

> I have no exclusive hold on the truth. Even though I have the Scriptures and the sacraments, I can still fail to see and understand and come to God through these channels of his word and grace in my Christian tradition. Other people, with much less, are able to discover God in deeper and purer ways. I have no exclusive hold on God, on his mercy and on his love, even though I am a minister of his Church. His grace, his love are gifts offered to everyone. These gifts are received and accepted in many ways, ways that I am often unable to see, let alone judge or condemn. I can only praise God and rejoice in the richness of his gifts.

May these homilies serve as a channel of grace for you in your journey through life.

Sharon M. Young
Editor

Does the One with the Most Toys Really Win?

TIME: NOVEMBER 29, 1987

SEASON: FIRST SUNDAY OF ADVENT

SCRIPTURE READINGS: ISAIAH 63:16B–17, 19B; 64:2–7;
1 CORINTHIANS 1:3–9; MARK 13:33–37

Someone should write a book on the theology of bumper stickers. When I was reflecting on today's readings on Advent, two bumper stickers came to mind: "In the end the one with the most toys wins," and "When the going gets tough, the tough go shopping." I don't think this is what Jesus meant when he told his disciples that they should be ready for the end. I don't think that what we have to watch for with a sharp eye is store sales.

No, I am not going to preach one more warning about the consumerism and commercialism of Christmas. Many of you already look for ways to avoid it, to preserve the spiritual dimension of Christmas in your life, in your home. I would like to raise the deeper question of our very style of life, of the way we live every day of the year, because I believe that what happens at Christmas is a reflection, a blow-up, perhaps, of our day-to-day life, of our ordinary attitudes and dispositions.

Lifestyle is one of those new words that everybody uses but that is almost impossible to define because everyone uses it in a different way. Some think of it in geographical terms and speak of, for example, a California lifestyle. Others associate it with age groups: "My lifestyle is different from my parents'." For many the word implies a different attitude toward sex, a permissive or promiscuous approach. Lifestyle is the manner in which individual persons, groups, and institutions go about meeting their needs.

> At its most basic level, human life is organized around the acquisition of food, affection, shelter, clothing, and health care. Around these basic human needs are the basic 'means' through which these needs are met: employment, transportation, education, recreation, and celebration . . . . [Personal lifestyle] includes that blend of tastes, habits and

practices which characterize a person's everyday behavior and relationships.[1]

There is an institutional lifestyle also, determined by the power structures and controlling interests in the group. This is the way people who are linked together—as a family, a religious group, or a political entity—work together to achieve certain objectives and interact among themselves and other groups.[2]

Lifestyle rests on certain assumptions about what is good or bad, right or wrong, fair or unfair, worthwhile or worthless, significant or insignificant in our life, in our world. Often these assumptions are not explicit, not articulated, but rather implied or subconscious. They operate below the surface of our awareness and conscious decision, yet they profoundly affect our life and destiny and that of others.

For example, much of our culture is based on assumptions: that bigger is better and that more is always desirable, that if it can be done it should be done, that might makes right, that no one can tell me what to do as long as I don't break the law or am willing to pay the consequences.

But there are even deeper and more hidden assumptions that underlie these, namely, that we live in a world of unlimited resources, that what works is what's right, that technology can solve all our problems, that the autonomy of the individual is the highest value.

What would happen if we were to reverse these assumptions, to live out of the conviction that the individual is an integral part of a whole, that we cannot be truly human except in the context of a community, that we exist in a web of relationships and are totally interdependent with one another, so that everything I do affects everyone else in the world and vice versa?

What would happen if we were truly convinced that our resources are limited and being used up at an alarming rate, that the spiritual, intellectual, emotional well-being of persons is just as critical as their material well-being, that the gross national product is not the only way (perhaps even the wrong way) to gauge the well-being of a nation?

These changes in our assumptions would profoundly change our lifestyle. They would begin to transform the way we think and feel, the way we work and spend our time, the way we speak and relate to one another, what we keep and what we give away, what we buy, what we eat and drink, what we are.

One way of getting below the surface in our lives, to see what our controlling values are, is to monitor how we spend our time and money. Keep a log of what you do for a month and see what it suggests. Itemize your expenditures for a year, when you prepare your income tax, and see where your money went.

During this Advent and even through Lent, I would like to suggest an alternative to the prevailing cultural lifestyle, a lifestyle that is an alternative to unthinking consumption, that is simple, that is responsible and caring for all the world, a lifestyle that is faithful, with a sense of stewardship to God and to Him who came "that we might have life and have it more abundantly." A lifestyle that is more Christian.

Why should we be concerned about lifestyle? If we are completely satisfied with the way we live, with the way things are for us and for the people we love, for the world in which we live, then there is no reason to change—and not much reason for Advent, because we have no reason to wait for, to hope for, a change. But today's readings suggest that we examine our values. The Gospel asks: When death comes, how will it find me? What will be important then—how many toys I have accumulated?

Paul tells us in no uncertain terms that what really counts in the end is Jesus Christ and our fellowship with him, the extent to which we have shared his life. Isaiah cries out in anguish, because the world is not the way it should be, not the world God intends, and we share responsibility for the shape it is in. And the Lord who comes to transform this world by his birth, and to transform our lives in the Eucharist, comes to us in humility, in the weakness of a newborn child, and in the simplicity of bread and wine.

Speaking Words of Comfort

TIME: DECEMBER 9, 1990
SEASON: SECOND SUNDAY OF ADVENT
SCRIPTURE READINGS: ISAIAH 40: 1–5, 9–11;
    2 PETER 3:8–14; MARK 1:1–8

On the first Sunday of Advent I suggested that the paradox of this season is not so much that we are supposed to be waiting with eager expectation for someone who has already come, but more that the one for whom we are waiting is in fact waiting for us, because it is in and through us that he comes into the present time and world. The Scripture readings for today suggest another paradox: We are both the people in need of comfort and the ones who are called to give comfort, to be comforters.

Try to imagine the state of mind, the feelings of the Israelites who found themselves exiled in a foreign land. Twenty, thirty, forty years have gone by. Hopes are dimming of ever returning home. Many of the original group have died. The young ones born as refugees and exiles in a foreign land are growing indifferent to the memories of the elders about a distant land and a national identity they have never known. They find themselves at home where they are. This is beginning to create tension, conflict, and division among the exiled community.

This kind of situation is not as far away in time and geography as the fifth century before Christ and distant Babylon (which is modern Iraq). I am told that this is what is happening to the Hmong, Laotians, and Vietnamese in our midst. The older generation is still hoping to be able to return home, while the young people are intent on making their way in the new culture. But in ancient Babylon, one of the exiles is called by God and told: Comfort my people, speak tenderly to forlorn Jerusalem, tell her that her time of suffering is at an end. And her children are about to come home! The exiles are called to give comfort to Jerusalem.

At the time of John the Baptist the people in Palestine were chafing under Roman occupation. Some were making the best of it, adapting themselves to the situation, accepting the new ways of the Roman culture that was trying to assimilate all conquered peoples. Others were secretly plotting terrorist acts and armed rebellions. The majority were probably trying to survive from day to day, wondering what would happen.

All of a sudden, out of the blue, this strange man comes out of the desert proclaiming that he is the messenger sent by God to prepare the way for the Lord's coming. The day of vengeance and retribution will be the day of liberation and restoration of the kingdom of God's glory. No wonder people are flocking to him from Jerusalem and all the Judean countryside!

As Christians, if we are really aware of who we are and who we are called to be, we are bound to feel ourselves, at least in moments of prayer and reflection, like strangers in a culture that is either indifferent or hostile to the values that we hold precious as disciples of Jesus, a culture that makes it difficult even for us to live by our values, a culture that tries to absorb and consume us and make us its own. I think this time before Christmas, which we are called to observe spiritually in the season of Advent, is one of the best examples of the conflict between our culture and our Christian ideals.

I don't know about you, but I find myself in need of being comforted, in my personal life and in my experience of the social and historical reality of the world in which we live. Personally, I feel strongly the limitations of time, the apparent temporariness of everything we know and do and are, the fragility of our plans and best intentions, the impossibility of reaching an unambiguous wholeness in the time at my disposal, the difficulty of being myself while trying to be for others.

And yet, here I am, called to speak words of comfort and hope for you and for myself. But this is not just my task as a priest. All of us are called to share the priestly and prophetic role of Jesus by reason of our baptism. Even if we are voices crying in the wilderness, we have to call our world to reform and transformation, to repentance and preparation for the coming of God's kingdom. The ministry of prophetic comforting is "to strive to interpret one's own times truthfully, to work to bring these times into line with the demands of God's final future."[3]

How do we do this? In my readings this past week, I found a suggestion about the Baptist's five "R's": remembering, returning, repenting, reforming, and reconciling.[4] John called his contemporaries to remember the great deeds of the Lord from the past, to remember the prophetic word, the great promises of God. He called them to return to the roots of their faith and trust in God, to faithfulness to his covenant. But in order to return they need to repent, to turn away from their sinful ways, to reform and change their lives according to God's word. And then they will be reconciled, they will find peace and unity in their relationships with God and with one another.

We are the messengers who are sent to cry out: "Make ready the way of the Lord!" We proclaim this message to ourselves and to the world. Prepare: our hearts, our homes, our communities, our world for the coming of his justice and his love. We call people to remember the waiting in hope, his coming in meekness and compassion, his dying in pain and his rising in glory.

We all need to return to the fervor of faith we once knew, putting God first, trusting in his power and not in the powers of this world; to repent of our ways of greed and selfishness and indifference to the needs of people all around us. We are called to reform our lives so that they will be in conformity with the values of Christ and the mystery of his presence within us. We are called not only to be reconciled, but also to be ambassadors of the reconciliation that God has entrusted to us in the death and resurrection of his Son.

I recently saw a poster that reads:

> For those who fear, time is too swift.
>
> For those who wait, time is too slow.
>
> For those who celebrate, time is too short.
>
> For those who grieve, time is too long.
>
> For those who love, time is not.

Perhaps that is the meaning of the eternity of God: For him who is love, there is no time, and "one day is as a thousand years and a thousand years are as a day" (2 Peter 3:8). For those who live in his love, there is no fear, and waiting becomes hope, and the celebration never ends, and grief is comforted by faith, and love is the victory that is in the making, the day of the Lord whose fullness is yet to come.

Comfort, give comfort to my people, says our God. Speak tenderly to our global village: Our servitude will come to an end, and our sinfulness will be overcome. The glory of the Lord will be revealed and all humankind, yes, all of us, Native Americans and European pilgrims and African American descendants of slaves; all of us, Arabs and Jews, Iraqis and Saudi Arabians and people of nations united, Palestinians and land settlers, we will all see it together and rejoice in it.

Bringing in the Year of Jubilee

TIME: DECEMBER 17, 1978
SEASON: THIRD SUNDAY OF ADVENT
SCRIPTURE READINGS: ISAIAH 61:1–2A, 10–11;
        1 THESSALONIANS 5:16–24; JOHN 1:6–8, 19–28

In my understanding of the meaning of Jesus, I would consider today's first reading from Isaiah as perhaps the key passage from the Hebrew Scriptures. The reason is the scene in the synagogue of Nazareth described in the fourth chapter of Luke, with which I am sure you are familiar. Jesus is in the synagogue on a Sabbath, and apparently he was already highly respected. He was asked to read and to comment on the Scriptures for that day. He took the scroll of Isaiah, he opened it to the passage we heard today, and he read it. Then he sat down, and all eyes were fixed on him as people waited to hear what he would say. He began by saying: "Today this scripture has been fulfilled in your hearing" (Luke 4:21).

This gives us a truly crucial insight, I believe, into the self-understanding of Jesus, and into the way he understood and accepted the great mission that the Father had given him. The way Jesus used this passage tells me that he deliberately chose to renounce the image of the Messiah-king, which was a legitimate image and a legitimate way of understanding God's working with his people, and to renounce the use of force and power over people, and instead he chose to see himself in the image of the servant who uses the powerlessness of the slave and the weakness of one who suffers.

There is a phrase in the first reading from Isaiah that is truly bursting with meaning in need of explication. The phrase says that the messenger comes "to announce the year of favor from the Lord . . ." (Isaiah 61:2). What that means is that the servant of Yahweh, the anointed one of the Lord, comes to proclaim a jubilee year. The jubilee year was intended to be the sabbatical of sabbaticals, the greatest of all sabbatical years. The sabbatical happened every seven years; jubilee was supposed to happen, therefore, every seven sabbaticals or forty-nine years.

The sabbatical is the idea of the Sabbath rest applied to the whole of creation, to the whole universe. The land was to lie fallow, and to rest. But there was more. Every seven years all debts were to be remitted. Every seven years slaves were to be given their option to be free, if they wanted to. And on the jubilee year, the land was always to return to its original owners, so that when land was sold, according to the law, the value was prorated in terms of how many years before the next jubilee year. This prevented anyone from accumulating large land holdings and keeping other people under their power. If a family became so impoverished that it had to sell its land, there was always the assurance that after a certain period of time they would be given a new chance, a new start.

It's hard to believe that kind of rule and law. What would happen to our life if we had that kind of sabbatical and that kind of jubilee year? I am sure you will not be surprised to hear that there is no evidence that the jubilee year was ever observed, even in Israel, or that the sabbatical year had any truly widespread and regular application. The jubilee year and the sabbatical year became ideals, became associated with messianic hope. The Messiah would bring the jubilee year. This is the ideal restoration that the Messiah would come to bring.

Think of that passage again with this in mind. Try to feel the tremendous impact of those words as Jesus read them and as he applied them to himself. He is sent by God, he is the anointed of Yahweh, he comes to proclaim good news to the poor, liberty to the captives, and to proclaim the jubilee year. The jubilee year is really going to happen now. The ideal is about to be realized and come true.

What does that have to do with us? A great deal, if we think of it this way: The jubilee year announced by Jesus and begun in him did not happen all at once. It is continuing to happen even now, and we are part of that happening. We also have been anointed and sent, in baptism and in confirmation. We are also sent to proclaim the year of favor. Among all Christian denominations and traditions, no one as much as the Roman Catholic Church and tradition believes that Jesus is alive and active in and through his people, that the historical presence of Jesus continues through his community of faith and love. More than any other Christian denomination or community, we as Roman Catholics have believed that we are part of this jubilee year. What does that mean?

Suppose you were in prison, in jail, and the door were to open and someone come and say: "You are free to go." If you had been dispossessed of everything you owned and someone came to tell you that you could have your possessions back, you could have your house back. If you were desperately poor and you were told: "This piece of land is yours now, you can work it and draw your sustenance from it." How would you feel? What would that do to you?

I think for most of us, it is almost impossible even to imagine what it means to experience this kind of radical change in our lives. There are people in our society who do know the meaning of it—people who have been set free from drugs, or from alcohol, or from destructive relationships; people who did find someone willing to give them another chance; someone who has received a gift that has enabled him or her to break out of the vicious circle of poverty, to gain some measure of control over one's life. I am sure there are many other similar experiences. If we in any way have been instrumental in facilitating this moment of freedom and liberation and this chance for new life for another human being, then we have been the messengers of God's salvation, and we have truly shared the gift that he has given us.

As far as our own feelings, if we have any sense of not being free, perhaps it is that frustrating experience of impotence that I think many of us have in the face of so much evil, so much corruption, so much abuse of power, so much self-seeking, so much destructive behavior at all levels of our society. We know this frustration and we see the signs of this sense of impotence and powerlessness beginning right now, in things like taxpayers' revolts, in strikes, in many forms of aggressive behavior between individuals and groups, as well as in new forms of escapism.

I truly believe that the message of the historical life and teachings of Jesus, whose final coming we still await, is the proclamation that we are set free from that kind of impotence, that we are not powerless except in a worldly sense, that we have the same transforming, renewing force that was in Christ Jesus: the love of the Father and his grace of salvation and the power of loving service.

We are *not* powerless, we are *not* impotent when it comes to our own life and our own attitudes and our own way of dealing with one another, when it comes to our circle of influence, no matter how small it may be. We *do* have the power to set people free—in our own families, for example, or in the circle of our friends—by limiting the demands we put on other people, by lowering our expectations of what we expect other people to do for us, and instead by raising our own willingness to serve each other.

We can set people free by being sensitive to the brokenheartedness and loneliness that is in people, and by offering the word, the gesture, the act of support; by supporting programs that promote justice and that truly help to set people free from poverty.

If the reality of the incarnation that we celebrate at Christmas time, if the gift of salvation from God our Father means anything at all, it means that we have been set free from sin and from the fear of death—but not just for our own sake. We are free *for* something. We are free so that we can work for a new world. We are free to make happen the time of joy and jubilee, which is God's gift in Christ Jesus.

The Sacrament of Listening

TIME: DECEMBER 20, 1981

SEASON: FOURTH SUNDAY OF ADVENT

SCRIPTURES: 2 SAMUEL 7:1–5, 8B–12, 14A, 16;
   ROMANS 16:25–27; LUKE 1:26–38

The Scripture readings today tell the stories of two immensely significant messages: one delivered to King David, and the other delivered to a young woman named Mary. David wants to build a temple to Yahweh, and Yahweh, through the prophet Nathan, tells him that it will be Solomon's task to build a temple. But that is not the important part of the message. Yahweh tells David that he, God, will build a house to David, meaning a kingdom of people, a nation that will endure forever.

Christian faith interprets that announcement as a reference to Jesus. In today's Gospel, the divine messenger states that the Son to be born of Mary will receive the throne of David his father, precisely the kingdom that is the object of the promise in the first reading.

Both messages are delivered in quiet moments without drama, without fanfare, without any kind of impressive display. God does at times reveal himself and his will in awesome manifestations of power. But he also speaks in the whisper of the breeze and in the moment of stillness and silence within. Especially when the fullness of God appears in the child born in Bethlehem, he comes very quietly.

Caryll Houselander, British author and mystic, writes in *The Reed of God:* "The Psalmist had hymned God's coming on harps of gold. The prophets had foretold it with burning tongues. But now the loudest telling of His presence on earth was to be the heartbeat within the heartbeat of a child."[5]

It's a good thing there was no Christmas shopping, or Christmas cards, or Christmas parties in Mary's time! The angel might never have been able to find her at home or to make himself heard to deliver his message. He would have a hard time finding me at home! But Mary was listening, and she heard the message. She answered, and she waited patiently for its fulfillment in the new creation that God fashioned in her. The faith of the Church speaks of Mary ever virgin. The idea of the perpetual virginity of Mary is a marvelous symbol that says to us that Mary was totally available and that she gave herself to God completely.

I believe that we must make ourselves totally available to God in order to be able to hear the good news and to welcome him. We need to be found waiting. We know the experience of waiting. Waiting in line reminds us of who is in charge, who is important. Nobody would make the President of the United States wait in line! Waiting at times is filled with the anxiety of the unknown. Why is a child so late coming home? Waiting is often part of the irritation of human relationships. Are you the one who is always late and rushing to get there?

The waiting of Advent is not something artificially imposed. It is an illumination of the experience of waiting. The discomfort of time, highlighted by waiting, is a dissatisfaction that God has implanted in our hearts, and Advent is a way through which God speaks to us and says: "Not yet! You are not home yet! This is not the kingdom as it should be! You have a way to go yet!"

We need to listen deeply within ourselves. What does it mean to believe in Christmas? To believe that God and the human are born together in this child of Mary? It means that God is a gentle love, a love that does not overpower but invites, a love that takes risks and invites, a love that is pure gift and invites, a love that allows us to refuse the invitation, and empowers us to answer, to accept it.

What does it mean to believe in Christmas? To believe that God's definitive approach to our life begins as a helpless child, born in questionable circumstances in a makeshift shelter, in a poverty that makes him a beggar? It means that God needs us, that he cries out to us in all who are in similar circumstances. You have heard that cry, and you have answered it in many wonderful ways.

Part of waiting is listening. We need to listen to each other. In many ways, when we listen to each other we are listening to God:

✛   *When someone is hurt and needs understanding*

✟ *When someone is angry and needs to express it*

✟ *When someone is happy and wants to share his or her joy*

✟ *When someone is alone and lonely and just needs another human presence and human voice*

✟ *When someone has written or read or found a poem or story and wants us to hear it*

✟ *When we come home broken and need to be put together again*

We need to speak to each other and hear each other's messages. How many things we want to say, and we never say them. How many words that need to be spoken never are voiced. How many feelings that should be communicated remain hidden, perhaps guessed, perhaps never even suspected. How many lives have been changed by the right word spoken at the right time. How many relationships have ended up broken beyond mending because the partners failed to communicate with one another.

We have only five days left before Christmas, and the pace of life is more frantic than ever. A few suggestions for ways to make the best use of those days:

✟ *Plan for a little time of silence, stillness, being available to God.*

✟ *Adopt an attitude of readiness to listen, being sensitive to other people's need to speak with someone who will listen attentively.*

✟ *Make an effort to say what needs to be said, to give the message that has been waiting to be delivered. Perhaps you can write it. At times we can write things more easily and better than we can speak them. Do you know anyone who has not had a good word or a compliment for a long time and could use one?*

The noise, the pressures both from within ourselves and from the world around us may be so great that it is difficult to hear each other, let alone listen attentively. But if we don't listen, we risk losing everything. If we don't listen to God, we may miss him completely when he comes to us. If we don't listen to and communicate with one another, our relationships either will not survive or will be very superficial. Let us make good use of the time at hand.

Happy Birthday, Dear Jesus

TIME: DECEMBER 25, 1975

SEASON: CHRISTMAS DAY

SCRIPTURE READINGS: ISAIAH 52:7–10; HEBREWS 1:1–6;
    JOHN 1:1–18

One morning, a few days ago, I was sitting alone in the little chapel trying to pray. It was already Advent, and my thoughts were focusing on the time of preparation and the coming celebration of Christmas. Perhaps, unconsciously, I was beginning to worry about this Christmas sermon. After all, can anything fresh and original still be said about Christmas?

While sitting there I was struck by a powerful visual contrast: the image of a child sitting on his mother's knee, reaching out to pet a little bird, surrounded by adoring angels, and right below it a crucifix, the image of a man on a cross, starkly white, ivory over dark wood, a man crying out: "My God, my God, why have you forsaken me?" And I was suddenly and sharply aware that they are both images of the same person, that the beautiful, peaceful child grew up to be the man dying on the cross.

And then I remembered having read recently, but where I could not recall, that Jesus is the only person who, when he celebrates his birthday, is expected and required to become a newborn child again, who every year when we attend his birthday party is represented and talked about as if he were an infant.

Can we celebrate Christmas and think of Jesus as he really is, an adult, bearing the signs of his suffering, present in our midst in the mystery of the resurrection life? Would this threaten the beautiful sentimentality of Christmas? Would this image destroy all the warm and tender feelings of this season? I don't believe that's possible, but, even if it were, I believe we should take the risk, because we cannot separate the child from the man.

We cannot build a truncated Christianity represented by the cute boy with curly blond hair of our childhood holy cards, and we distort the meaning of Jesus if we do not let ourselves be confronted by the challenge of his full human life.

So I invite you to celebrate a birthday, the birthday of Jesus Christ, the Son of God. We have all that we need for a party: beautiful decorations, lots of happy people all in a good mood, candles burning and gifts without number, some already shared and others still brightly packaged, and visions of tables heavy with good wine and delicious food.

But where is the guest of honor?

He is here, he is truly here. He is with us because we believe in his word. He will be with you in your family gatherings when you call upon his name, when you think of him with love. He is not here as a newborn child, but he is here as the Risen Lord, he who has lived our life, and preceded us in death, and gone before us into new life, and calls us to follow him in a life of service, and in death as the final act of self-possession and self-surrender to a loving Father, and through death into the mystery of a fuller and richer life.

He is here in the care and kindness and patience, in the sympathy and compassion, in the acceptance and support we are able to give one another, because then we act as he would act and we fulfill his command to love one another as he has loved us.

He is here, not as one for whom life is finished, and for whom nothing new is possible and all goals have been attained, but as one who is fully alive and still growing, an active participant in our process of looking ahead and setting goals and working to achieve them.

What does a birthday party say, what does it celebrate? Why do we give parties for those whom we love? Because we want to say: We are happy you were born. We are happy you are here with us. We rejoice in the fact that life has brought us together, that in a variety of ways you are part of us, that you share our being and our living, that we have been given the unique gift of knowing you personally.

Our good wishes say to the birthday person that we believe life still holds promises and hope and that there is more life to live, more joys to share, more challenges to meet, more evil to overcome, more good to realize—that there is more of us that is yet to come, both separately and together.

Are we willing to celebrate Christmas as the birthday of a man who challenged the whole world and the whole of history to a new vision and a new life, a man willing to die on a cross for his convictions and his mission?

It is easy enough to welcome into our homes and our churches a warm, cuddly, sweet little baby. But beware, because that baby grows up to challenge and reverse many of our values. Can the immensity of the demands of Jesus find room in our lives, or must we forever keep him as the lovable but innocuous little child and call that Christianity?

If we are willing to accept Jesus in the wholeness and integrity of his life and death, to welcome him in faith as the risen Son and the Lord of our life, then let us celebrate his birthday with joy and laughter, with song and celebration, with gifts of bread and wine shared in communion. For it is Christ's Mass, the joy of all our todays, the hope of all our tomorrows.

The Importance of Being Family

Time: December 30, 1984

Season: Feast of the Holy Family

Scriptures: Sirach 3:2–6, 12–14; Colossians 3:12–21;
    Luke 2:22–40

Members of a good family are intimately involved with each other. They share everything, ups and downs, happiness and grief, successes and failures. That is what family is about.

About a year ago, a charming and extraordinary boy died. He was known to the public as "David." I am sure you will remember him. For almost his entire 12 years he lived in a plastic bubble. His system had no natural immunity to disease and, despite every human effort, modern medicine could not save him. His death was as astonishing as his life. He winked at his doctor and asked simply to be allowed to go home. He did not appear to feel sorry for himself, to rant or rave. He spent his last hours holding his parents' hands, something he had not been able to do very much before. For all of his 12 years David was a remarkable boy, and everyone who encountered him attested to his extraordinary qualities.

But David was not born with this extraordinary sensibility and goodness. He could not have survived or become a beautiful human being without his remarkable parents and all the people who in caring for him became tied to him by bonds of love and deep affection. Love supported and nourished David—the love of his parents and of the extended family that developed around him. The reverse is also true. David's parents and all those around him were changed forever as a result of his life. He had an enormous impact on all who loved him.

The same thing is true of Jesus. Many of us have a hard time understanding what that really means. We grew up with the impression that Jesus came forth from his mother's womb with all the qualities of a perfect human being, with all the goodness, the holiness, the virtues, of the Son of God. Not so. If that were true, Jesus would not be human as we are human.

To be truly human, Jesus had to receive, as well as to give. He was deeply influenced by his parents, but his extended family, by his environment, by his culture. Joseph and Mary did not feed only his body; they also nourished his soul and spirit, they contributed to the development of his personality in the same way that our parents contributed to and influenced our development.

The Gospel reading today makes an eloquent statement about the love and tradition, the forces and influences that shaped Jesus and nourished and supported him as he was growing in size and strength, in wisdom and grace. Mary and Joseph are there, Simeon and Anna representing the prophetic tradition and the people's longing for salvation, and the law that brings his parents to the temple, and God whose presence is hidden in the temple's holy of holies.

Of course, not only the lives of Mary and Joseph, Simeon and Anna, but the lives of millions of other human beings have been changed because of this child. For some he is light and salvation, for others division and controversy. Those who are family to this child, in whatever age, will know the warmth of his love, will have to face his challenge and radical demands for a new way of life, will receive the gift of his peace. Jesus has become an integral part of our world, of our world of interdependence and relationships that form the web of our life, the very stuff of our existence and of our becoming.

What difference does Jesus' presence in our world make for our family life and relationships? What can we learn from the immediate family of Jesus for the life of our families? Paul, in the second reading from the Letter to the Colossians, seems to summarize and bring together what he has learned and experienced about the meaning of Christ for human relationships. He speaks of heartfelt mercy, kindness, humility, meekness, patience, forbearance, forgiveness, love, gratefulness, peace, instructing and admonishing one another, doing everything in the name of the Lord.

I am sure none of us want to or can take exception to any of these qualities of life. Perhaps we are so familiar with these concepts and admonitions that they fail to make a real impact in our life. What would our life be like if we really lived the way Paul directs?

Paul speaks first in general about life in the Christian family. When it comes to the question of family life, he does not seem to see it any differently than the culture of his time, or the prevailing teaching of the Stoic school of philosophy. Husbands and fathers are the authority in the house, and the well-being of the family rests on the submission and obedience of other members to him.

If we hear it that way, we fail to grasp the revolutionary meaning of the teaching and example of Jesus. John Howard Yoder, an outstanding Mennonite theologian who teaches at Notre Dame University, in a book titled *The Politics of Jesus*, argues very persuasively that this and similar passages of Paul are in fact calling for the radical change in relationships embodied in the life of Christ.

Christ did not impose any kind of violent shift in relationships within the family and society. This is the revolutionary demand of the ethics of Jesus: that the one who is thought to be greater must subordinate, put himself or herself under the other, must put himself or herself at the service of the other. Because he who is the Word through whom creation came to be, who is the Lord of all and the King of the universe, who shares in the very glory of God, humbled himself and became a servant to his creatures, subordinated himself to his subjects, so we his disciples are called to subordinate ourselves willingly to one another, to serve one another, especially if we have been given some position of authority.

If we probe beneath the cultural and historical crust of the Scriptures to see how we might be able to understand this passage of Paul for today, we might hear something like this:

> Husbands and wives, always put each other's needs before your own. This is your duty in the Lord. Love one another. Avoid any bitterness, any anger, any resentment. Children, with respect, learn from your parents. Listen intently, imitate them in following the Lord. Parents, support and challenge your children only in love. Always set them free, give them heart.[6]

Whatever we do, for each other, with each other, to build our families, to strengthen our human relationships, to nourish and feed, to challenge and instruct, to cherish and love one another better, we must do it in the Lord. He is very much part of all our relationships. He is part of our family. He is involved intimately with each of us. He shares our happiness and grief, our successes and our failures. If we are able to share our faith in him, our love in him, our families will grow in holiness, will know his peace.

The Gifts of the Magi

TIME: JANUARY 3, 1988

SEASON: EPIPHANY OF THE LORD

SCRIPTURE READINGS: ISAIAH 60:1–6; EPHESIANS 3:2–3A, 5–6;
   MATTHEW 2:1–12

We are just concluding the Christmas festivities, but the Church is already inviting us to look forward to Easter, as we are instructed to announce the date of Easter on this day. This is fitting, for there would be no Christmas celebration without the death and resurrection of Jesus. In a sense, whenever we come together to worship and celebrate the Eucharist, we renew the whole mystery of Christ, so that we may become part of it, and incorporated in him.

Father Raymond Brown has described the infancy narrative in the Gospel of Matthew as a "gospel in miniature," because it includes the whole sequence of revelation, proclamation of the good news of salvation, and the two-fold reaction of acceptance and rejection. "The gospel is good news, but that gospel must have a passion and rejection, as well as success."[7] Today's Gospel speaks of acceptance by the Magi and rejection by Herod. In the rest of the chapter, Jesus is taken to Egypt because his life is threatened. Innocent children are killed. But Jesus will return from Egypt and fulfill his mission.

> In the persons of the Magi Matthew was anticipating the Gentile Christians of his own community. Although these had as their birthright only the revelation of God in nature [as the Magi who had followed the star], they had been attracted to Jesus; and when instructed in the Scriptures of the Jews, they had come to believe in and pay homage to the Messiah.[8]

Christian piety in subsequent centuries continued to interpret and adapt the story to different situations. For example, the gifts became symbolic of the doctrines about Christ that had become explicit in the creeds: gold to honor Jesus as king, incense to recognize Jesus as God, myrrh, a burial spice, to confess Jesus as Son of Man who was to die for our salvation. But the gifts also became symbolic of the different aspects of the believer's response to God in Jesus Christ: gold symbolizing virtue, incense symbolizing prayer, and myrrh symbolizing suffering.

How can we interpret and adapt the story of the Magi for ourselves and for our times? The story has three things to say to me, in my spiritual life, and I would like to share them with you.

The first is that our search for God never ends, certainly not as long as we are earth-bound and immersed in this history, which is still only on its way toward completion. This means that I can never be satisfied and become complacent. I can never rest even when I think I have found God. I can only rejoice in those precious moments of discovery. I must always remember that there is more to God than what I have been able to meet and experience.

The second point that speaks to me in the story is the symbolizing of the gifts as a description of what I must bring to the Lord.

Virtue. The gift of gold symbolizes those habits of the heart, those habitual ways of thinking and feeling and acting that shape me into the kind of person the Lord has called me to be. I need to grow daily in virtue so that, habitually, my response to every situation is shaped by my faith in Jesus Christ, my hope in his power of new life, my love for him and for all with whom he has identified himself. These virtues or gifts include:

Prayer. The gift of frankincense reminds me that I need to come to the Lord more and more with the prayer of the heart, a prayer that allows the silent and mysterious presence of God within me to become not just one of many realities, not only one idea, one intellectual assent among many others, but rather the one and only reality with the power to give meaning and content and direction to all that I do, to my whole being.

Suffering. The gift of myrrh reminds me that suffering of one kind or another, at one time or another, is part of every human life. I need to understand more and more that while there is a dark and painful side to suffering, there is also a redemptive, transforming, liberating, purifying side to it that enables me to be associated with the suffering of Christ and prepares me for a deeper union with him.

The third point is that I want to be able to respect the search and the journey of other people, the different ways in which God reveals himself to different persons. I have no exclusive hold on truth. Even though I have the Scriptures and the sacraments, I can still fail to see and understand and come to God through these channels of his word and grace in my Christian tradition. Other people, with much less, are able to discover God in much deeper and purer ways. I have no exclusive hold on God, on his mercy and on his love, even though I am a minister of his Church. His grace, his love are gifts offered to everyone. These gifts are received and accepted in many ways, ways that I am often unable to see, let alone judge or condemn. I can only praise God and rejoice in the richness of his gifts.

To Christ who was, who is, and who is to come, the Lord of time and history, be endless praise for ever and ever.

Baptized into Community

TIME: JANUARY 10, 1988

SEASON: BAPTISM OF THE LORD

SCRIPTURE READINGS: ISAIAH 42:1–4, 6–7; ACTS 10:34–38;
　　MARK 1:7–11

Our celebrations of Christmas and Epiphany have empha-
sized the fact that Jesus is the incarnation of God for all
people and for all ages, the man for all seasons and all nations.
This affirmation should not obscure the fact that Jesus was
born a Jew, not as some abstract form of human being, unre-
lated to the time and place of his birth. The paradox is precisely that this human being, in all the concreteness and par-
ticularity and limitation of his historical reality, has become
the norm of all that is human, God's saving presence and power
for the whole of creation.

Biblical studies have brought out more and more clearly
that Jesus was a Jew of his time, affected by his culture, deeply
rooted in the traditions of his people, in the thought and language patterns of his time. His ministry was directed primarily to his own people, and he challenged the religious leaders of
Judaism to understand the mystery of the God of their fathers
and of his saving love for his people in a new way.

The genealogies of Matthew and Luke are intended to
establish beyond all doubt that Jesus is of the people of Israel
and a descendant of David. Although there are a few instances of
Jesus dealing with non-Jews, they are usually connected with
statements affirming that his mission is primarily, if not
exclusively, to the people of Israel.

One way to interpret the story of the baptism of Jesus is to
see it in this context, as a powerful statement of Jesus' relationship to the people of Israel. Jesus responds to the call to
repentance being proclaimed to Israel by John the Baptist, he
responds as a pious and devout Jew, and he is revealed as the
Messiah expected by the Jews, God's servant-messenger, God's
beloved and unique Son.

In the Gospel of Mark Jesus is identified from the opening verses as the faithful servant of Yahweh whose suffering

will bring life to many. The language of today's Gospel passage implies the language of the first reading, the first song of the suffering servant in Isaiah. The baptism of Jesus affirms his intimate connection with his people, with their ancient traditions and with their present conditions.

The baptism of Jesus becomes the basis and the model of Christian baptism, of the rite by which we become identified as disciples of Jesus and incorporated into his community. I would like to make the same point about our own baptism that I have made about the baptism of Jesus.

There is no such thing as a universal Christian community, untouched by historical developments, unaffected by circumstances of time and place. There is no such thing as an abstract, pure Christian baptism. There is no person who is just a pure, simple Christian, independent of the historical development of Christianity. We are Roman Catholic and Lutheran and Reformed and Anglican and Evangelical and Pentecostal Christians, and so on.

By our baptism, we were incorporated into a specific, historical community of Christians, with specific, deep, strong traditions, ways of interpreting and living the mystery of Christ, that make us different from other Christian communities. We belong to the Roman Catholic Christian tradition. We have a proud, extraordinary, unique history of both sinfulness and grace. We have a distinctive endowment of rich gifts, as well as regrettable mistakes and excesses and blunders. Both the glory and the shame are ours. They belong to us, and we belong to each other and to our history and to our ancestors, just as any family does.

In recent years we have grown tremendously in our ability to understand and to respect other historical traditions and forms of Christianity. We have learned to accept each other in the fundamental faith we share in the one God and one Lord, Jesus Christ. Generally we accept each other's baptism and do not re-baptize children or adults who want to join our community, but we do ask them to accept what we are, what we believe, what we celebrate and how we worship, our history and traditions.

Just as we are open to people from other Christian traditions who want to join the Roman Catholic Christian community, so we understand that a Roman Catholic may decide to join another Christian church. But it should be a decision made with much reflection and prayer, because a person has become convinced that God is calling him or her to a different experience of God's love in Christ Jesus—not just because we like one preacher better than another, or because of the warmth of the people or the quality or style of the music.

I am afraid that in some ways we are not clear ourselves about what it means to be a Roman Catholic. In the great renewal experienced by the Catholic Church in the past twenty-five years, we have lost some of our sense of history, of our feeling for our distinctive character, and of our loyalty to the community, to the family to which we belong because of our baptism. We need to recapture this sense of belonging, of identity, of loyalty as Roman Catholics, while retaining our newly acquired critical sense toward our own institution and our ecumenical acceptance and respect for other Christian churches.

Two weeks ago a young couple from Italy visited me for several days. The husband is the son of some old and good friends. He and his wife came to California for a visit following their recent marriage. The days they spent with me made me realize how deep are my roots in my Italian origin. I have lived twice as long in the United States as I did in Italy. I am an American, and I speak Italian with an American accent, but in many ways I am also still Italian, and I care passionately about Italy, its successes and its failures, its cultural and artistic achievements, its many political, social, educational, and economic problems.

I feel the same way about being a Roman Catholic. I love the Catholic Church passionately, and I really believe that I have been faithful and loyal to the Church, even or especially when I find myself forced to disagree and to dissent. I wish I could share more this loyalty and this pride and this gratitude with you. Just as Jesus, by his baptism, affirmed his roots in Israel and Judaism, so we by our baptism belong to one of the unique branches of God's family on earth, of his historic people. This is what we celebrate today in word and sacrament.

Why Go to Mass?

TIME: JANUARY 14, 1973
SEASON: SECOND SUNDAY IN ORDINARY TIME
SCRIPTURE READINGS: I SAMUEL 3:3B–10, 19;
      1 CORINTHIANS 6:13C–15A, 17–20; JOHN 1:35–42

Why do you come to Mass? Personally, I wish the law of the Church that states the obligation of going to Mass every Sunday would be removed and forgotten. How many of you would have stayed home today? I don't mean to imply that acting out of obligation is bad or worthless, and even if the law of the Church were abrogated we would still have the law of God to keep holy the Sabbath, or the day of the Lord. We do have a basic need, rooted in our experience of contingency and dependence, to recognize and express our relationship with God. But there are many ways of doing that.

It seems to me that there are two very compelling reasons for coming to Mass on Sunday. First, what happens here cannot be duplicated or achieved in any other way: the gathered community and the encounter with the extraordinary, personal presence of the Lord in the Eucharist. Second, we have been personally invited, called, just like Samuel and the first disciples were.

I felt this invitation when I was studying in Berkeley—even daily, although I did not always find the experience I was looking for, like Samuel. Besides the personal invitation that is expressed through the need I experienced to be with other Christians in prayer and celebration, just wanting to be there when I knew they were gathering for the Eucharist, I also feel an historical call that has come through the ages. We read that after the Ascension, "All these, with one mind, continued steadfastly in prayer with the women and Mary, the mother of Jesus, and with his brethren" (Acts 1:13f). After Pentecost, "The Christians continued steadfastly in the teaching of the apostles and in the communion of the breaking of the bread and in the prayers" (Acts 2:42).

Here we see the beginning of the custom of daily reunion in private homes where, in an atmosphere of joy, of divine praise and prayer, the Eucharist was celebrated during a fraternal meal. The daily gathering is portrayed as the privileged place and sign of the profound unity that ruled the community. The community assembly actualized the Church and in some way identified with it.

In his first letter to the community at Corinth, Paul writes that the unity of the believing Christians is like the unity of a living body, the body of Christ which is the Church, expressed in the unity of the bread in which all Christians communicate. The body of Christ is at the same time both the body in which we communicate and the body of the Church of which we are a part. To divide the Church by breaking the unity of the assembly is to destroy the body of Christ. For Paul, the assembly is not just any gathering; it is the Church itself, the body of Christ, and every offense against the assembly is an offense against the Lord's body.

The first Christians seem to have considered the assembly extremely important. They remained faithful to it despite the lies the pagans circulated about their gatherings, despite pressures and persecutions. During the persecution of Diocletian, the martyrs of Abitina told their judges: "We cannot forgo the assembly of the Lord's Day. The Lord's assembly cannot be interrupted."

Every assembly, not only Sunday's, is a feast, a common manifestation of the Church's joy. One of the particular purposes and effects of the assembly is to aid each of its members to support in himself or herself the faith and hope which are the source of a Christian's joy. Each member of the assembly brings to it his or her own contribution by profession of faith, fraternal presence, and the witness of his or her unshakable confidence.

In Matthew's Gospel we read that Jesus said: "Where two or three are gathered together for my sake, there am I in the midst of them" (Mt. 18:20). The Church Fathers used this passage to describe ecclesial, churchly gatherings. The presence of Jesus in the assembly is a constant theme. The assembly is the body of the Lord animated by his Spirit. In the assembly the Church realizes and fully manifests itself, in the visible presence of the faithful and the invisible presence of the Spirit of Christ.

The Syriac *Didascalia,* written in the second half of the third century, expresses this very powerfully:

> Teach the people by precepts and exhortations to attend the assembly without fail: let them always be present, let them never diminish the Church by their absence, and let them never deprive the body of Christ of one of its members. Each should take as for himself, not for others, the words of Christ: 'He who does not gather with me scatters' (Mt. 12:30; Lk. 11:23). Since you are members with Christ, you must not be scattered outside the Church by neglecting to come together. In short, since Christ our Head fulfills his promise by becoming present and entering into communion with you, do not despise yourselves and deprive not the Savior of his members; rend not his body nor scatter it.[9]

Vatican II and contemporary writers repeat the same theme. The same call, the same invitation is still proclaimed today; through the centuries, it reaches us. This is why I feel that the liturgy, the celebrations of our community, have priority of time, energy, and resources.

Our Common Priesthood

TIME: JANUARY 24, 1988
SEASON: THIRD SUNDAY IN ORDINARY TIME
SCRIPTURE READINGS: JONAH 3:1–5, 10; 1 CORINTHIANS 7:29–31;
    MARK 1:14–20

I think the second reading from 1 Corinthians needs a few words of explanation, even though it is not directly related to the other two readings. These three verses, taken out of context, do not seem to make much sense. The whole chapter seven is devoted to advice to the married, to the unmarried, about marriage to unbelievers and about divorce.

Two things must be kept in mind. In the first place, Paul believes that he and his fellow Christians are living in the last season of the last age, and that that season is nearly over. For Paul, this was the last generation, and the urgency of the coming of the end suggests that the only important matter is to serve the Lord, not to worry about one's status or other worldly matters. Second, Paul makes it very clear that what he is saying is his own opinion, not the command of the Lord. He is confident that he can make reliable applications of the good news he has received, but he is not imposing an obligation on all believers.

When seen in this context, the second reading fits into the general theme of the urgency of God's call to turn to him and to serve his kingdom, to accept the total character of our Christian vocation. It is not just a call to Sunday worship or to an occasional good deed. It is a call to live our whole life in the light and in the power of Christ.

I would like to return to the notion and the reality of the priesthood as the best way to express the total life quality of our Christian vocation. Today I want to stress the magnificent reality of our baptismal priesthood. This is a concept that the Roman Catholic Church has rediscovered and embraced again wholeheartedly in the last thirty to fifty years. At the time of the Council of Trent, because the Protestant Reformers insisted on the priesthood of all believers in such a way as to deny the need for the ordained priesthood, the Catholic Church reacted by emphasizing the essential difference between the two, rejecting the position that everyone in the Church "without distinction" can do everything, and giving such prominence to the ordained priesthood that the priesthood of the faithful was hardly ever mentioned.

One of the results of our ecumenical dialogues, one of the most important elements of Christian faith that we have brought into full light again as a result of the challenge received from the Protestant tradition, is this wonderful doctrine of our sharing in the priesthood of Christ by our baptism. Here is the foundational statement of the Second Vatican Council on the common priesthood:

> Christ the Lord, High priest taken from among men, made the new people a 'kingdom of priests to God the Father.' The baptized by regeneration and the anointing of the Holy Spirit, are consecrated as a spiritual house and holy priesthood, in order that through all those works which are those of the Christian . . . they may offer spiritual sacrifices and proclaim the power of Him who has called them out of darkness into His marvelous light. Therefore, all the disciples of Christ, persevering in prayer and praising God, should present themselves as a living sacrifice, holy and pleasing to God. Everywhere on earth they must bear witness to Christ and give an answer to those who seek an account of that hope of eternal life which is in them.[10]

The Council, while upholding the need that everything in the Church be done with due and decent order, and while resisting any reductionism whereby the ordained priesthood would simply be absorbed or "subsumed" in the other, also affirms the unity of the priesthood of the faithful and the sacramental priesthood as a "participation in the one priesthood of Christ." It speaks of the sacred power of the ordained, but also affirms the power of the faithful by reason of their common priesthood.[11]

Not only bishops and priests, but all of God's people stand under the apostolic mission to teach and proclaim the Good News of Jesus Christ. The right and duty of all the baptized to participate in the apostolic mission of the Church is not something received by delegation from the ordained ministers, but is derived from the union of each member with Christ, the Head of the Church.

Lay people are not mere witnesses or respondents in the celebration of the Eucharist, but active participants. You offer your gifts and spiritual sacrifices, your service, your life not *through* me as the ordained priest, but *with* me. And the lay people are called to exercise their ministry, to use their gifts, their individual calls to service both in the Church and in the world. What we have in common, as sacramentally ordained priest and as baptized people, is far more fundamental, far more extensive and decisive than what distinguishes us. In the language of the council, the distinction is a "diversity of service" that exhibits an even deeper "unity of purpose."

I thank God that so many of you have understood this truth of your priestly role and have heard the Lord's call to ministry in the Church and in the world, and have answered it with generous and faithful dedication in so many different ways. More and more men and women are doing full-time pastoral ministry. But the great bulk of service in the Church is still done by volunteers. Look at the liturgical ministers, altar servers, lectors, Eucharistic ministers, those who assist with music and welcoming.

Think of all the people involved in catechetical ministries, in sharing their faith and proclaiming God's word and God's love, in building communities of faith with our children and young people. Think of all the people who are taking more and more responsibility in the administration and organization of a parish or diocese, providing resources and direction for the community. Think of those who make themselves available to support and encourage one another in marriage, or at the time of crisis and separation, by death or divorce. Think of those who spend time in ecumenical dialogue and activities, in promoting issues of social justice and peace, or in health care, and in so many other ways.

Where would the Church be without the emergence of this growing consciousness and commitment of every member of the community to the various forms of pastoral ministry? The Church has always depended on volunteer ministries. What is new is the understanding that apostolic service is the right and the duty, the privilege and the responsibility, of every baptized person. Each of us is called to our special vocation in the midst of God's people: like Jonah, who was called to preach in Ninevah, even though he did not want any part of it and ran away; like Simon and Andrew and James and John, who left everything to follow Jesus.

All of us are called by Jesus to continue conversion, to change our minds and hearts, to receive the Good News of God's love and salvation, to live under the reign of God, to share the Good News, and to help in the building of his kingdom. This is our common priestly vocation.

The Voice of Authority

TIME: FEBRUARY 3, 1991
SEASON: FOURTH SUNDAY IN ORDINARY TIME
SCRIPTURE READINGS: DEUTERONOMY 18:15–20;
    1 CORINTHIANS 7:32–35; MARK 1:21–28

Few prophets are remembered for having uttered those great words: "Have a nice day!" or "Go with the flow!" Certainly not the Hebrew prophets. In the Hebrew and Christian traditions, the prophets are the ones who are not afraid to go face to face with God and to fight the demons within us, to hear God's thundering voice and feel his consuming fire, to get into a shouting match with the dark powers in our life.

The promise made by Moses in the first reading is fulfilled and surpassed in Jesus who, in the Gospel reading, is beginning to teach and act with authority. The promise is rooted in the fear of the Israelites and in the role of Moses. The Israelites in the desert, confronted even from a distance by the presence and revelation of God in the great mountain storm, were afraid and did not want to get any nearer to God.

> Now when all the people perceived the thunderings and the lightnings and the sound of the trumpet and the mountain smoking, the people were afraid and trembled; and they stood afar off, and said to Moses, 'You speak to us, and we will hear; but let not God speak to us, lest we die.' . . . And the people stood afar off, while Moses drew near to the thick darkness where God was. (Exodus 20:18–19, 21)

Ancient peoples believed that no human could survive coming face to face with God. In these passages from Exodus they ask Moses to act as their intermediary with God, and this is the reference we heard in the first reading. God accepts the people's reverential fear and awe, and not only works through Moses but also promises another great prophet like him, who will bring forth the words of God.

The original meaning of this passage referred to the prophetic tradition as a whole, to the succession of the great prophets of Israel. With the end of prophecy in Israel, about four hundred years before Christ, the passage came to be understood in reference to the coming of the great day of the Lord that would initiate the destruction of the wicked and the victory of the just (see Mal. 3:23–24; 1 Macc. 14:41). It was then that Elijah would return, and/or a prophet of the stature of Moses would arise to prepare the day.

And now Jesus appears on the scene. He teaches with authority and holds his audience spellbound. The prophets who had come before would preface their remarks with the words: "Thus says the Lord," but Jesus begins his utterances by stating categorically: "I say to you." And his words are not empty words. They are effective, they cast out the evil power and bring about healing, revealing the saving presence of God.

Jesus' words pass the test set up in the verses that follow today's first reading from Deuteronomy: his words come true, his word is fulfilled. Jesus, the holy one of God, has power over Satan, is able to overcome the power of evil. And after the resurrection the disciples came to realize that Jesus was even greater than Moses. He was not just an intermediary, a messenger for God, but the real personal divine presence and power at work in their midst. No wonder he could speak and act with such authority that all were amazed and astonished, even though they did not fully understand who he was.

Paul speaks with the authority that he has received as an apostle of Jesus Christ, but in the seventh chapter, from which today's reading comes, when he is talking about marriage and celibacy, he is very careful to distinguish between what the Lord commands and what he, Paul, is recommending. He is evaluating the situation of his own time and trying to determine the better course of action in the light of God's revelation in Jesus Christ. His perspective is that the end is coming soon, "the world as we know it is passing away," as we heard in last Sunday's reading. With a very pastoral and caring heart, Paul is trying to suggest what he thinks would be best for his fellow Christians, without imposing his interpretation on them.

In our historical situation, without the pressure and urgency of an imminent end to life and history as we know it, I think we would see things differently. I hope that the experience of all married people is that your love for each other is not a distraction and an impediment for your love of God, that you are not divided between your love for wife or husband and your love of God, that you are able with, in, and through each other, to give yourselves entirely to the Lord.

Separated by many centuries and many miles we are still spellbound by the words of Jesus and his authority. We still feel with amazement the power of his presence in our life, because he is truly in our midst as the risen Lord. But we still need the prophetic voices of our time to interpret the teachings of Jesus and to help us fit those teachings to the circumstances of our life.

Who speaks to us with authority? To whose voices do we listen? Whom do we trust and follow? President Bush and the Pentagon briefings? The Pope? The National Conference of Catholic Bishops? Individual bishops, like the twenty-nine members of Pax Christi USA who recently issued a special statement on the situation in the Persian Gulf? Dorothy Day or Daniel Berrigan? Jean Vanier or Mother Teresa? Theologians like Cardinal Ratzinger or Charles Curran? Papal statements on human sexuality or *Playboy/Playgirl/Penthouse*?

To whom do we go to educate and form our conscience so that we might be able to recognize in the depth of our being, in our heart, the authoritative teaching of Jesus, the will of God for us? When all is said and done, that authoritative word of God, that personal call to saving faith and holy life, must be experienced and acknowledged in the mystery of our own heart and conscience. But we cannot shape our conscience according to God's word all by ourselves, without some help from others.

And who will act with authority in our life? Who will exorcise the demons of our day? Our demons are as powerful as those Jesus confronts in the Gospel readings. There is no doubt in the Gospel of Mark about the power of demons or the authority of Jesus. Perhaps we are not so sure, and we need to be reminded that the power of evil is still very much alive and active in our world, and that only the power of God can overcome it.

Making Sense of Suffering

TIME: FEBRUARY 7, 1982
SEASON: FIFTH SUNDAY IN ORDINARY TIME
SCRIPTURE READINGS: JOB 7:1–4, 6–7;
        1 CORINTHIANS 9:16–19, 22–23; MARK 1:29–39

Did you think it was strange, did you feel a little uneasy, when the reader concluded the first reading with Job's cry of despair: "I shall not see happiness again!" and we answered: "Thanks be to God!"? It would be rather difficult to thank God if we had all the troubles of Job. He had lost it all. His children, servants, and possessions were gone, and their loss made no sense. He had contracted some loathsome disease and was out on the dung heap, and he had done nothing to warrant all this suffering. His friends showed up armed with all the religious clichés of the day, but Job would have none of it.

We can learn a lesson here. It is almost blasphemous to apply religious clichés like Band-Aids to someone else's pain. More is accomplished by sitting with the sufferer than by attempting to rationalize suffering. Job's religious advisers sat with him, speechless, for a week at the sight of his condition. They were probably more comfort to him then. When they started speaking, they alienated and infuriated Job because they were trying to convince him that it was all his fault, that he was being punished for his wrong-doings. Job keeps insisting that he is innocent, that he does not deserve the suffering he is in.

Then there is Job's wife. She is also a big help. Unwilling to accept his protestations of innocence, she offers the ultimate answer of the cynical: "Curse God and die!" She helps us understand the choices clearly. Without hope in God, there is only one alternative—hers.

Job discovers that looking for a rationale, a reasonable explanation for his situation, is a dead-end street, filled with ashes. Job cannot accept his wife's alternative, either, because he cannot let go of God. His last choice: to go back to God with his complaint. Overwhelmed with his loss, filled with depression, Job clings to God. He argues, complains, is bitter, questions God, but through it all he maintains his relationship with God.

In the end, this relationship becomes deeper and stronger, when he lets go of his self-righteousness and accepts the mystery of God.

Today's first reading was chosen to set the scene, to raise the question. The Gospel is the response, a powerful response to the anguished human cry, like Job's, that is such a part of our human condition. The answer is Jesus, the Risen Christ. Who is this Jesus we see healing Simon Peter's mother-in-law and others, casting out demons who know who he is?

There is no question that the historical Jesus worked miracles and exorcisms. This was not unusual for that time. What was problematic was the meaning of such actions. Wondrous activity immediately raises the question: What do those works tell us about the person who performs them? In the Gospel of Mark, the identity of Jesus is constantly misunderstood by both enemies and disciples.

Today's reading implies that Simon and his companions saw Jesus only as a wonder-worker, tracking him down so that he can work more miracles. But from the experience of Jesus as dead and raised from the dead, from the perspective of resurrection faith, Jesus' true identity is discovered, and Mark shares that faith with us. Jesus is a man united with God in prayer. He has come to proclaim the Good News of God's salvation. More than that, he himself is the Good News.

Jesus worked miracles or performed exorcisms to show that God's kingdom was beginning in him, and that his actions and his words signaled the breakthrough of God's salvation in this world. After the resurrection, all that Jesus had said and done was seen in a different light. He is not just acting as God's envoy, he is God's saving power. He is the healing presence of God, he is God's Son, victorious over all the powers of evil—even the power of death.

Jesus rejected the people of his own time who thought that religious clichés and obedience to religious rules could ease the suffering and the misery of the world. The crowds grasped at him, hungry for insurance against the sickness and dementedness of daily life. He healed and he comforted. When he was overwhelmed by all this suffering and meaninglessness, he turned to his single source of hope: his relationship with God. He went off to pray. And he had to face his own suffering, meaningless beyond imagining. Yet his continuing trust that none of this was beyond God's dominion gave him a hope that would sustain him beyond death.

Jesus and Job were sustained in the end because they refused to give up their hope in God, even in the face of the mystery of evil. In the end, Job's question about justice in life was answered by Jesus' life. Job could find no notion of justice except in this life. Jesus' unwavering trust in God—in death as well as in life—opened to all of us a new hope: resurrection to eternal life, trust in a loving God who can change even death into new life.

When all ties to the future seem cut off, when our suffering, pain, hardship appear to have no meaning, when we find ourselves immersed in a hostile, threatening world, we are faced with Job's choice. We can curse God and die, or we can come to God with open hands and hearts, bound by a hope anchored in the Holy One, Jesus the Christ. When we do, God breathes a mysterious and gentle comfort in the whirlwind of our lives.

When we do, we can even begin to be the wounded healers, like Jesus, whom our world needs so much. In an old Talmudic legend, the Messiah is at the city gates. In response to the question, "How shall I know him?" the legend states: "He is sitting among the poor covered with wounds. The others unbind their wounds all at the same time and then bind them up again. But he unbinds one at a time and binds it up again, saying to himself, 'Perhaps I shall be needed. If so, I must always be ready so as not to delay for a moment.'"

We need to bind our own wounds in hope, so that we will be ready when we are needed.

We're All in This Together

TIME: FEBRUARY 14, 1988
SEASON: SIXTH SUNDAY IN ORDINARY TIME
SCRIPTURE READINGS: LEVITICUS 13:1–2, 44–46;
  1 CORINTHIANS 10:31–11:1; MARK 1:40–45

In the light of the Gospel reading it seems very hard to understand the first reading from the book of Leviticus. If any person was unclean, because of circumstances over which they had no control, they were excluded from the worship and from the social life of the community. "To be unclean was to lack holiness, and such was viewed not as a moral condition but as a state of being incompatible with the holiness of Yahweh and hence prohibitive of any contact with him."[12]

Integrity was demanded of the Israelites in their relationship with God. Because God is holy, all his people must be holy. Holiness meant wholeness, integrity, being without blemish or disorder or ugliness or anything unclean. That is why lepers, or anyone with any visible skin disease, were to be excluded from the community: Their presence defiled the community. Exclusion was equivalent to death, especially in ancient times. Physical survival was almost impossible, and without human relationships there is no truly human life.

> Further, God is known and worshipped in community; expulsion from it means expulsion from the only place one can meet the creator and redeemer of all life. Without this encounter, human beings are only living corpses—the walking dead. The rabbis considered lepers 'living corpses' whose cure was equivalent to resurrection. And it was in fact a resurrection, since healing brought the outcast into the community where communion with human beings and God could occur, i.e., where one could live, as opposed to merely existing.[13]

A physical illness, therefore, made a person a social and religious outcast. It is hard to conceive of a God who demands this kind of holiness, who rejects the sick who are most in need. Jesus turns this attitude upside down. He touches the leper and brings him healing. He breaks the barrier between clean and unclean, and he does it with the authority of God.

The God who is in Christ Jesus reaches out to the sick and the outcast, to make them whole, to incorporate them into his people.

How do we react to people who are sick, who lack wholeness in our society? Do we still go by the rules of the book of Leviticus, or do we live by the spirit of Jesus? How do we really feel about people with AIDS? Would you visit a person so afflicted? Would you help to take care of him or her? Do you remember the story of the two hemophiliac boys in Florida who contracted AIDS through blood transfusions? They were driven out of school and out of the community when their home burned to the ground under mysterious circumstances.

Recently in our local newspaper there was the story of a practical nurse who takes care of three severely handicapped persons. He takes them to Woodward Park, and in the story he told of the negative, hateful reaction he gets from some people. There seems to be a strong feeling that such people who are not "normal," by our definition of the term, should not be seen in public, should be kept in institutions or in homes.

Do we follow Leviticus, or do we follow Jesus? Our translation says that Jesus was "moved with pity," but the Greek word in the more ancient and preferable reading states that Jesus "was angry." It is not only pity or compassion that is asked of us as disciples of Jesus. We also need to be angry about the way many of God's children are treated.

It is part of the genius of Roman Catholicism to insist that the community is absolutely essential for our relationship with God, for our growth in holiness, wholeness, integrity. Even the great prophetic figures who seem to stand alone and apart are called by God from the community and sent back to the community with his word of challenge and reproach.

We need the community, the Church, and the Church needs us. That is why, if we have cut ourselves off from God by our sinfulness, if we have turned away from God and walked in a direction that distances us from him, when we turn back to him we need also to turn back to the Church. We need to be reconciled to the community, just as the leper was sent by Jesus to present himself to the priest, to the representative of the community.

In the past we thought that just about everything we did wrong was a mortal sin, and that we had to go to confession almost every time we went to communion. Today we realize that a mortal sin is only that change of fundamental attitude that truly separates us from God. It is a change in the fundamental choice that we make for our life: to live with God, or to live without God. It does not happen lightly or casually. But if it does happen, we need to go to the priest in confession, perhaps not so much to be forgiven by God, because I believe God's response to our sin is to forgive, but to be assured of and to celebrate that forgiveness by being reconciled to God's holy people, by being welcomed back by the community from which we had turned away, as we had turned our back on God, by being invited again to receive the Eucharist, the great sign of our communion with God and with his people.

We need the community of God's people for our growth in faith and hope and love. The season of Lent, upon which we shall soon embark, is an invitation to a serious commitment to this spiritual growth. We cannot do it alone. I invite you to share this springtime in preparation for the new life of Easter with your fellow believers. I know I find tremendous support in the people who gather for daily Mass and for our special Lenten programs.

I find inspiration and encouragement in your faith, in your desire to be more intimately united with the Lord, to live a life more completely centered in God's will and love. Your presence tells me that I am not alone, I am not cut off, that I belong to God's holy people, and that the Lord is with us. He is with us now as together we offer him our longings and desires, our gifts and our service, our Eucharist.

Accepting Forgiveness

Time: February 18, 1979

Season: Seventh Sunday in Ordinary Time

Scripture Readings: Isaiah 43:18–19, 21–22, 24b–25;
    2 Corinthians 1:18–22; Mark 2:1–12

Again today the Gospel reading presents Jesus to us in the act of healing. But this time the healing goes deeper than legs immobilized by paralysis. It reaches the very heart of the person and heals his sinfulness. The person is made whole not only in body but also in mind and heart. In the passage from Second Isaiah, the people are in exile in Babylon. That exile, which had been interpreted as God's punishment for the sins of the people, was about to end.

The words of Isaiah were spoken to a people who were looking back to the marvelous things that God had done for them in the past, especially to their deliverance from Egypt and the Sinai covenant, the first exodus. The people were asking: Where is our God now? Why does he not act?

Isaiah's message to the people is that something new was about to happen: a new act of deliverance, a new journey through the desert. It is time to return home, to return to the land of the promise in a new exodus. God has wiped away all their offenses. He no longer remembers their sins. It would be the same as if someone said to us today: "All your troubles are over, a new age is about to begin. All your mistakes are forgotten and made right."

Do we know how to forgive one another? Can we say: "Your sins I remember no more!" to someone who has hurt us, offended us, done wrong to us? It is one of the most difficult things to do. Perhaps this is the reason we are so reluctant to believe that God can and does do that with us, that he wipes away our offenses, that he says to us—as Jesus said to the paralytic in today's reading—"Your sins are forgiven," that he remembers our sins no more.

How do we know that? Jesus Christ reveals the mercy and forgiveness of God in his words and in his actions. The purpose of the incarnation, of God's manifest presence in Jesus, was precisely to take away our sins.

The second reading has a marvelous statement that presents this truth in a striking way: "As surely as God is faithful, our word to you has not been 'Yes and No.'" For the Son of God, Jesus Christ, whom we proclaimed among you . . . was not 'Yes and No'; but in him it is always 'Yes.' For in him every one of God's promises is a 'Yes.'" Jesus is the divine "yes," spoken to us with all our weaknesses and problems, faults and failures, sins and sinfulness.

Where do we meet the compassion of our God? How do we hear the words of forgiveness spoken to us personally: "Your sins are forgiven"? In many ways, I am sure. When we cry out to the Lord for his mercy, and can find peace. When we pray together, as a community, "Lord, have mercy." When we experience the intimate encounter with our saving Lord in the holy Eucharist. When we gather to hear the word that proclaims the compassion of God.

From the beginning there has been a sense that the community had a role to play in the process of forgiveness. Various forms developed throughout the history of the Church. The most recent change, just a few years ago, gave us the option of going to confession face to face or remaining anonymous. It is very simple: You have the choice. The most significant and also the most difficult change is not in the rite but in the attitude, in the approach—an attempt to confess not only what I have done, but who I am and where I stand before God, what fundamental choices I have made for my life.

It was hoped that the new rite would encourage more people to use the sacrament, to celebrate in this way the great mystery of God's mercy and forgiveness. This has not happened. I can tell you from experience that it can be one of the most effective means of personal, spiritual growth and development. It is the meeting point, the moment of encounter between our repentant heart and the mercy of the Father.

There are times when we need to share this experience with one another, times when we need the proclamation of God's forgiveness through the representative of the community that we believe to be the continuing presence of the saving, forgiving Christ. We need to celebrate the mercy and forgiveness of God through the sacramental sign that makes it real and active for us, in our life, in that moment of grace.

Perhaps we, too, are paralyzed because we cannot forgive ourselves. We need to trust God's word of forgiveness spoken to us. We need to believe that he remembers our sins no more.

Going into the Desert

TIME: FEBRUARY 25, 1979

SEASON: EIGHTH SUNDAY IN ORDINARY TIME

SCRIPTURE READINGS: HOSEA 2:16B, 17B, 21–22;
    2 CORINTHIANS 3:1B–6; MARK 2:18–22

Have you ever thought of the desert as an ideal place for a honeymoon? I often ask newlyweds where they plan to go for their honeymoon, and no one has ever told me that they were going into the desert, or camping in the Sierra wilderness.

The prophesy of Hosea, in the first reading, must be heard as a call from Yahweh to his people, Israel, to return to the place of their first encounter of love, to the place of their honeymoon. For Israel the desert was the place of God's intimacy. Describing honeymoons, one commentator states:

> Honeymoons are privileged times to celebrate, free from all distractions and everyday practicality, the unrestrained joy and love for life vowed to one another in the face of an uncertain future. Newly married husbands and wives retreat to the mountains and shores not so much for the mountains and shores as for the opportunity to be alone with one another and to revel in that privileged time of exclusive self-giving to one another. God calls the people into the desert to free them from every human support and concern that can distract them from the divine self-giving, which is the ultimate source of all life. Human weakness demands that we be emptied so that we might be filled with God's bounty.[14]

Hosea is speaking to a sinful and unfaithful people God's word that summons them away from the cities of their sinfulness to the stark and bare desert where things are simple and straightforward, where choices are few and clear-cut, where it is easier to judge what is important and what is not, to determine what means life and what means death. Because it was in the desert that Israel first met God.

Moses was the first to encounter the holy presence in the burning bush. There he met the God of his fathers and God's demanding will to save his people. Israel, led by Moses, ventured forth into the unknown desert to find the God of their freedom, and they met him at Sinai. In the desert they were tested by God, and they dared to put God to the test. They came to know each other and to trust each other. Yahweh took them as his people and they accepted him as their God, just as husband and wife take and accept each other.

The desert was the privileged time of their love, and for centuries to come there was a nostalgia for the purity and intensity of that experience. Often reforming groups would establish communities in the desert to isolate themselves from the corruption of life and to make themselves open and receptive to God's presence and action.

In the Christian era, even to this day, there are monks and other individuals who choose the desert as the place of encounter and communion with God. Some of the spiritual movements today suggest a practice called "a day in the desert." This means a day, or whatever portion of a day one can manage, spent in the mountains or another place of solitude and silence, by oneself, away from civilization, without books or other aids, to be by oneself in prayer and reflection. I have only done this a couple of times, but I found it profoundly renewing.

But the desert is really more a state of mind, an attitude, than an actual place. The city is a place of richness and comfort and pleasure and abundance of material goods, but we must pay for that with a loss of liberty and consuming toil. The desert is the place of letting go of the superfluous, getting down to bare necessities. The desert is the ability to see things clearly, to know what the real values are, to know what is important and what is not.

The desert is a place where our strength and endurance, determination and dedication are tested. Relationships with other people, friendship and trust, are particularly tested when people journey together in desert places. Yahweh and Israel journeyed through the desert, Yahweh testing Israel's fidelity and Israel testing Yahweh's patience. But while the desert is unforgiving, God forgives. The people of Israel recognized that they survived the desert because God had carried them in his arms as a father carries his child (Deut. 1:31). The desert, then, is the attitude of complete trust and fidelity.

The prophet Elijah ventured into the desert alone seeking a new vision of God by which he might restore his faith and his courage. He discovered God in the sound of silence. The desert is a search for silence and inner stillness so that we might hear God's whisper. The desert is many other things, and we will continue to explore those things during our Lenten season, which we will describe as our journey into the desert to meet the living God, to renew our covenant, our life with him.

Today's word is simply an invitation to take the season of Lent and Easter very, very seriously. It is not just a desert, but also springtime in the desert, when all the vital forces are building up and getting ready to bloom into new life. New life, new growth, sinking our faith roots deeper, an explosion of vigorous faith, bearing new and more abundant fruit, is what we seek during this season.

How do we create the desert within ourselves? Fasting may be one way of experiencing the meaning of desert subsistence in our bodies. Getting up early in the morning, before the city is awake, making use of that stillness for our reflection, coming to early Mass to hear God's word in the stillness of the morning before being assaulted by the demands of the day. Finding other moments of stillness and silence for personal prayer, for being alone with God, for finding peace. Helping others on the journey by giving support to those who are weak, steadying those who stumble, sharing our food with the hungry and our water with the thirsty, encouraging one another.

Above all, I hope that taking Lent and Easter seriously will mean that we look very carefully and very honestly at what is important and what is not important in our life, for our journey. When it comes down to a question of life and death, what and whom do we ultimately value? Are we willing to follow God's lead into the desert, even though the road is uncertain and the future unknown, and the desert full of fears? Even though we think we know another way, easier and better?

If we are to be made new, to share the new life of the Easter Christ, the Risen Lord, we must be willing to let go of our security and complacency and accept the risk of a desert journey with God.

A Time for Discipline

TIME: FEBRUARY 17, 1988

SEASON: ASH WEDNESDAY

SCRIPTURE READINGS: JOEL 2:12–18; 2 CORINTHIANS 5:20–6:2;
    MATTHEW 6:1–6, 16–18

Discipline is an essential part of any decent, happy, fruitful human life. All of us knew discipline as children: the discipline imposed on us by our parents, including proper habits of eating, cleanliness, sleep, self-control. We learned that we could not have everything we wanted whenever we wanted it. In school, our teachers taught us the discipline required to be on time, to be quiet or speak as appropriate, to do our homework.

As we grew up into adolescence, into young adults and mature persons, we came to understand more and more the need for discipline in our lives, for the survival of the community, for the best use of our energies and talents and time. We were able to internalize what before had been controls imposed from outside and to make self-discipline, self-control, our own intelligent, personal choice. It is possible to exaggerate discipline to the point that it destroys all spontaneity and creativity, but I think that today the more prevalent problem is the lack of understanding and practice of discipline.

Lent is an annual reminder of this need for discipline and self-control in our life, in our spiritual life, in our life of loving union with God. The Gospel reading has just given us the teaching of Jesus on the three major, traditional disciplines of the spiritual life: prayer, fasting, and almsgiving. They are more than specific actions; they represent a way of living.

Prayer has to do with the need to give an adequate time to the Lord. The Lord deserves our prime time, not just a quick moment snatched here and there, before falling asleep, while driving a car, when suddenly we need something from him. The goal is that our whole life will be lived with the Lord who is at the heart and the center of our being, in a growing consciousness of his presence and will for us.

Fasting has to do with our ability to control the material things that are so much part of our life, rather than being controlled by them. These include such things as food and drink, cigarettes, television, money and possessions, ambition and power, seeking our happiness in material pleasures to the extent that we forget that our true happiness can be found only in the Lord.

Almsgiving is more than a dollar or two, or even ten or twenty given to the homeless or the starving. It is an attitude of continuing concern for the needs of our brothers and sisters, a willingness to do what we can so that every person is treated justly and has a chance to live a decent life.

None of these practices of discipline are ends in themselves. They are not just exterior practices, as Jesus made poignantly clear in today's Gospel, but they must correspond to our interior selves. One commentator put it this way:

> The season calls us to restraints—to step away from the immediate complexities of our lives in order to see more clearly, with a deeper perspective, what is going on in the daily imperatives that seem so easily to take control and to deny us a stewardship of ourselves. The need for Lent corresponds to a basic requirement for spiritual growth: we need to step back from the appetites and responsibilities that obscure our vision. . . .

> Lent is a God-given opportunity to rediscover the priorities by which we want to live. We need space in our lives, space that will permit us a greater clarity of vision, a deeper insight into how the faith we profess must find authentic expression in our daily lives. . . . The yearly return of Lent invites us to identify with those who suffer by freely accepting restraint and self-denial, but not for the cultivation of a self-centered piety. If I read the gospels correctly, this is where Jesus tells us the connections [that] must be made: restraint and self-denial are to be a source of liberation from self to free us for the service of others, especially for the service of human beings whose lives are a perpetual Lent.[15]

Once again we are invited by the Lord, through the Church, to the observance of a holy Lent: to repentance and faith, to the rediscovery of how God is calling us to turn to him in faith and to express that faith in the service of others, in the love and by the power of him who became a servant for our sake, obedient unto death, even death on a cross.

Taking Part in the Story

Time: February 21, 1988

Season: First Sunday of Lent

Scripture Readings: Genesis 9:8–15; 1 Peter 3:18–22;
Mark 1:12–15

In the mind and in the faith vision of the biblical writers, the beginnings of human history are a growing and deepening process of sin and evil—from Adam and Eve to the moment when God cannot stand it any longer and decides he had better start all over again. The waters of the flood return the earth to the chaotic conditions from which it first emerged, but what comes out of the flood is something new and greater, the first explicit covenant of God with his material and human creation, a covenant extended to all, by which God binds himself to keep the process going, not to destroy his creation again.

The Christians to whom the First Letter of Peter is addressed are experiencing a time of crisis and trial. They are dispersed through the pagan world, living in small communities, threatened by persecutions. The text we read is an attempt to give a theological rationale for enduring suffering and tribulation. As Jesus was put to death but also given new life in the realm of the spirit, so the baptized can hope to escape the time of trial by being given a share in the resurrection of Christ.

Jesus is put to the test in the desert for forty days, but he emerges victorious. What seems to be another tragedy, the arrest and death of John the Baptist, becomes the beginning of a new era, the beginning of the fullness of God's time, proclaimed by Jesus as the coming of the reign of God.

How does it happen that a disastrous flood turns into the beginning of a new cosmic relationship between God and his world? How does it happen that a man crucified like a criminal between two thieves is raised from the dead and proclaimed Lord of all? How does it happen that a small group of followers of this crucified Jesus, without power or resources, also persecuted and put to death because of their faith in Jesus Christ, grows into a worldwide movement with a tremendous impact on the course of history?

It happens as gift and grace, by the involvement of God in human history, because the power and the goodness and the love of God are constantly at work in the struggle against evil and all destructive forces that threaten God's creation. We call this the history of salvation. It is a way of expressing our faith that God shares our battle against darkness and death and evil, and that his goodness will win, his kingdom of peace, justice, and love will prevail, that the day will come when there will be no more tears, no more death, no more mourning, because God will make all things new according to the vision of harmony and beauty that he has for the world.

We believe that the history of salvation has unfolded through the history of a people, through the incarnation of the Son of God by which God became physically, concretely, visibly, personally part of our world, and that this history continues to unfold through the active, saving presence of the Risen Christ in the world and in his people, in his Church, in everyone who lives out the reality of God's kingdom which he preached and lived. The history of salvation is a continuing story: It is our story.

Lent is the retelling and reliving of this story so that it can become more immediately, more consciously present to us, so that we can become more thoroughly engaged in the making of this history. Do you want to be part of it? Do you want to be part of God's salvation, to be able to accept it fully as a gift for yourself, to share it with others as an instrument of God's saving activity in the world? Live the season of Lent, live the telling of the story of God's merciful and gracious love.

How? In the mythical story of the flood, Noah did what God asked him to do: He built the ark so that life could continue. What was he really asked to do? He was asked to keep the process going, to preserve what should not be lost, to help save all that could be saved in the face of impending destruction.

What is there in our time, in our world, that God wants us to save and preserve? What can we do to help avert the disasters that threaten our natural environment, our human survival? What can we do to save and protect human life, and all life, to overcome hunger and disease and violence, to preserve those precious values and ideals that give meaning and dignity and quality to human life?

Perhaps there is something in our homes, in our work situation, in our immediate communities that needs to be changed—in the way we treat one another, in the way we consume and waste, in the way we isolate ourselves and remain indifferent to the destiny of our brothers and sisters.

Jesus had to take time in solitude and prayer in order to confront the difficult choices of his life and the reality of evil, to be able to remain open to the challenging and sustaining presence of God. If even Jesus requires this time, how much more do we! Very few of us can find the time and the opportunity to spend even one day in the desert. But somehow we need to find time to be alone with God, to be totally present to him in prayer, to reflect, to reassess where we are before him, time just to be with God. I know I could not survive, or do what I do, without solid, faithful time in personal, private prayer as well as communal prayer, especially the celebration of the Eucharist. Make time for prayer during Lent.

The reading from the Letter of Peter draws an awkward comparison between Christians saved through baptism and Noah and his family who were saved from the flood. The writer wants to emphasize that baptism is more than a removal of sin: It brings about a whole new consciousness in the hearts of believers; it is the beginning of a new life. And because baptism is a participation in the death and resurrection of Jesus, it is the key to understanding and enduring the trials and tribulations that are part of every life.

If Jesus, the Son of God, had to suffer and die, so will we. But it is not just for the sake of suffering. It is for the sake of the transformation of suffering into joy, of death into life, proclaimed by the resurrection. This is the very heart of the history of salvation. Suffering has tremendous redemptive significance, and by the power of God it will turn into the new and glorious moment of salvation.

What is there of darkness and sin in our life that needs to be redeemed? What is there of death that needs to be changed into new life? What is there of pain and suffering that needs to be understood in the light of the redeeming death and resurrection of Jesus?

Lent is an invitation to die to our old selves, to enter into the passion of Jesus by our own suffering, so that we can be part of his new life, so that we can become that new creation that is the goal and the promise of the history of God's salvation.

The Meaning of the Cross

TIME: MARCH 3, 1985

SEASON: SECOND SUNDAY OF LENT

SCRIPTURE READINGS: GENESIS 22:1–2, 9A, 10–13, 15–18; ROMANS 8:31B–34; MARK 9:2–10

Do you find it hard to believe in a God who asks a father to offer his only son in sacrifice to him, even if it turns out to be only make believe, only a test? I do, and I need to look for explanations, for interpretations that say that the story reflects our way of understanding the mystery of God and what God asks of us, not the way God really is.

The exegetes, the Scripture scholars, explain the story as a rejection of the Canaanite practice of human sacrifice. Traditional Jewish commentary on this passage maintains that God already knew the fidelity of Abraham but gave him the opportunity to express the generosity and goodness that was potential in him. For Abraham to sacrifice Isaac was to surrender the grounds for all his hope, for all his future, into God's hands. Jews refer to the Genesis story as the "binding of Isaac," and the experience of persecution and suffering has made the story a metaphor for all that the Jews have endured because of their faithfulness to God and to the Law.

The Christian articulation of the story sees in the son's obedience unto death the image of Jesus' willing acceptance of death as a sacrifice for the salvation of the world. Paul, in the second reading, cannot but think of that, allude to that, when he reflects on the death of Jesus and extols the generosity of a God who does not spare his only Son, his beloved, who does not hold back what is most dear to him: Jesus, who is uniquely his Son, as the Gospel reading makes brilliantly clear.

Is that any easier to believe, a God who sacrifices his own Son, who wills the death of his only begotten Son, for the sake of a humanity steeped in sin, for the salvation of the world, so that I can be saved? I confess that I find this even harder to accept and understand. And so again I look for explanations, as Christian believers have done from the very first disciples to those of today.

There is no question that Jesus is truly God's only Son, the Father's beloved. The Transfiguration offers a pictorial expression of the transition in the perception of the followers of Jesus from seeing him simply as a good and gifted and prophetic man in their midst, to the recognition of the mystery of divine presence and power at work in him.

When this good, gifted, holy, prophetic man died on the cross, his disciples asked why, what does it mean? From their experience of faith, the disciples answered: Jesus died because of our sins, because of the sins of the world.

Christian faith has proclaimed for two thousand years that Jesus is uniquely God's son and that he died because of our sins and for our salvation. I believe that we must affirm this faith, if we want to be faithful to the way God revealed himself in this man Jesus, and to the original, normative, experience of faith. But when it comes to further understanding and explanation and interpretation, we have had theories of expiation and sacrifice, of redemption and ransom, of justice and retribution, of atonement and reconciliation, of substitution and debt payment.

I believe that forgiveness is God's response to human sin from the very beginning. I believe that reconciliation comes from the infinite, compassionate love that God has for us, a love revealed in the whole history of salvation. I believe that Jesus embodied the immense mercy of God and revealed his forgiveness in his dealings with sinners.

I believe that Jesus died on the cross because he was faithful and obedient to the task that the Father had given him of proclaiming the reign of justice and love, of peace and reconciliation for everyone: the little ones and the despised, the poor and the outcast, even the sinners and the enemies. This put him in mortal conflict with earthly powers and authorities that eventually put him to death.

I believe that the death of Jesus on the cross signifies and reveals for all generations the extent of the power and tragedy of sin and its terrible consequences. This man who is the ideal of what it means to be human, totally innocent, a model of justice, compassion and love, who restored health to the sick, sight to the blind, life to the dead, hope to the poor, is put to death because of misunderstanding, jealousy, fear, hatred, manipulation, lies, religious intolerance, self-interest. The litany could continue. We know it well; it is part of our daily life.

I believe that the Father raised his beloved Son from the dead to show us that his love is stronger than our hatred, his goodness stronger than our evil, his mercy stronger than our sinfulness, his life-giving power stronger than our killing.

Because we all share in the mystery of sin and evil, we are called to make our own Christ's victory over sin and death, to know deep in our hearts and with our whole being the forgiveness, peace, reconciliation, new life that the Father has revealed and offers us in the life, death, and resurrection of his beloved Son.

We are invited to see ourselves, to examine our life, in the shadow of the cross and in the light of the Transfiguration. In the shadow of the cross we experience the depth and the tragedy of our sinfulness. In the light of the Transfiguration we meet the Risen Christ, the ultimate pledge that God will hold nothing back from us, that he offers us the fullest reconciliation and the most intimate and enduring love.

The Bare Minimum

TIME: MARCH 10, 1985

SEASON: THIRD SUNDAY OF LENT

SCRIPTURE READINGS: EXODUS 20:1–17; 1 CORINTHIANS 1:22–25; JOHN 2:13–25

A contemporary psychiatrist has written: "So long as a person lives under the shadow of real, unacknowledged, and unexpiated guilt, he . . . will continue to hate himself and to suffer the inevitable consequences of self-hatred. But the moment he begins to accept his guilt and his sinfulness, the possibility of radical reformation opens up, and . . . a new freedom of self-respect and peace."[16]

Paul, in his attempt to understand the history of God's salvation, begins with Abraham's faith, his act of complete trust in God, about which we heard last Sunday in the story of Isaac. Then he looks at the Law given in the Mosaic covenant, the Law read to us again today, as a step that became necessary later, because of human sinfulness, so that we could see our transgressions and be convinced and convicted of our sins: "No human being will be justified in his sight by works of the law, since through the law comes knowledge of sin" (Romans 3:20).

Father Champlin, in his excellent book *Together in Peace,* on the sacrament of penance and reconciliation, uses the Ten Commandments as one of the ways to look into our heart, to examine our life. He calls it "the bare minimum." The Ten Commandments are good guidelines for decent human life. If we live by them we are good human beings. We are not Christians, yet, but at the same time it is rather evident that we cannot be good Christians without also being good and decent human persons.[17]

If, during this Lenten season, we are serious about conversion, about change of heart, about getting in touch with the reality of our sinfulness and turning wholeheartedly to God to receive his forgiveness and to be reconciled to him and to one another, then we cannot avoid taking a serious look at our life in the light of these basic rules of human living. We do not have time for a detailed analysis of the meaning of the Ten

Commandments for our age, but I would like to suggest some lines of reflection.

The first commandment presupposes that the Jews had the choice of other gods. We also have the choice of the ultimate value in our life, the first priority, the final loyalty: Who, or what, is number one in our life? God must be number one. No created being, nothing shaped by our hands or technology, no fad created by our image makers, can take the place of God. He is a jealous God, jealous of his place of absolute importance in our life.

The second commandment asks: How do we use God's holy name? Does it come to our lips with respect and love, do we use it to call on him in times of need and pain, when we want to share our joy and give him praise? Do we use it without thinking, as an exclamation to punctuate our speech? Do we use it to bolster our lies and to justify our injustice and to support our violence? Do we design and name our gods to fit our needs and our limits?

What does it mean to keep holy the Sabbath? We have put so much emphasis on going to church on Sunday that we have forgotten what the commandment says. It talks about rest, the need to stop our frantic activity and to take time for ourselves, time to nourish our minds, our spirits, our imagination; time to nurture our relationships with God, with our families and friends, with ourselves. This commandment was intended to protect the slaves from being worked to death, from exploitation, from being regarded as instruments of production. It implies regard for human needs and dignity.

The fourth commandment is addressed to a community of adults, not children, and is meant to protect the elderly at a time when some nomadic cultures simply abandoned those who had become a burden, leaving them in the desert to die. The question of the proper care for the elderly who are unable to care for themselves is one of the most difficult and troublesome of our time, as the miracles of medicine extend life longer and longer.

"You shall not kill." It seems a simple and straightforward injunction, but how many theories and interpretations have been developed over the centuries to justify wars, capital punishment, abortion, violent revolution. I very much like the metaphor used by Cardinal Bernardin of Chicago. He spoke of a consistent ethic of life as a seamless garment covering all issues that affect life from the womb to the tomb, that calls for a respect for life that includes concern for the quality of human life and includes questions of hunger and destitution along with war and abortion.

A group of third graders was asked to write down the commandments. For the sixth, one wrote: "You shall not commit adulthood." Another wrote: "You shall not admit adultery." The original commandment did not exclude the practice of polygamy; it was primarily a question of justice and rights that were not to be violated, rights that belonged mostly to the man. Over the centuries it has come to include all questions of sexual behavior. In a world that looks at sex as a pleasurable bodily function, not much different from sitting down to enjoy a good meal, how do we hold on to an ideal of sexuality that sees genital sex as the sign and the reality of the total gift of one person to another, in a stable, permanent and loving relationship, open to the mystery of being called to participate in the creative, life-giving power of God?

Commandments seven, nine, and ten have to do also with respect for the rights and integrity of others—for the sacredness of a person's home, the need for one's personal life and relationships, even within the context of a larger community. In what ways do we do violence to each other in these aspects of life? It is not only the work of burglars and muggers.

The prohibition against false witness has less to do with everyday lying than with the distortions of truth that can prevent someone from obtaining justice.

When I read the Ten Commandments at the first level of understanding, as a list of things that I am supposed to do or not do, I feel pretty good. I am doing well. But when I read them in a reflective manner, as I have done with you today, I feel I should bow my head in shame for all that I have failed to do to promote the values of human life and dignity that are expressed and proclaimed in these laws. And that is only the bare minimum!

As a Christian, I am asked to go farther, to proclaim, to follow, to imitate the total self-giving love of Christ crucified. In him is the wisdom and the power of God. In him is the salvation of the world.

The Real Meaning of John 3:16

TIME: MARCH 13, 1988

SEASON: FOURTH SUNDAY OF LENT

SCRIPTURE READINGS: 2 CHRONICLES 36:14–16, 19–23;
  EPHESIANS 2:4–10; JOHN 3:14–21

Today's Gospel contains what is probably the most quoted verse from the entire Bible. There is hardly a televised sports event or parade where one does not see somewhere a large sign saying "John 3:16." And we just heard that verse. "For God so loved the world that he gave his only Son, that whoever believes in him may not die but may have eternal life." It is one of the most beautiful statements in the Scriptures, and probably the best one-verse summary of our Christian faith. But verse 17 should always go with it: "God did not send his Son into the world to condemn the world, but that the world might be saved through him."

From my experience with people who are fond of quoting John 3:16, I have a feeling that what they really want to say is contained in verse 18: "Whoever believes in him avoids condemnation, but whoever does not believe is already condemned for not believing in the name of God's only Son." That wraps everything up in a neat little package: Either you believe in Jesus or you don't. If you believe in him, you are saved. If you don't, you are condemned. Since the person quoting the verse is usually a believer, he or she is implying to somebody else that they are not saved because they don't believe in Jesus, or don't believe in Jesus the way the Scripture-quoter believes.

It is very dangerous to take a couple of verses out of context, to read them so literally, and to pass judgment and to condemn two-thirds of the world with those verses. I *do* believe that the world is saved through the incarnation and the death and resurrection of Jesus. I *do not* believe that everyone who does not believe those specific historical events is condemned.

These verses must be understood in context. In the Gospel of John, in the context of the repeated biblical affirmation of the universal salvific will of God, and in the context of a passage like Matthew 25:31–46, the great scene of the last judgment as described by Jesus, when all the nations, meaning everyone, are gathered before the throne of judgment for the division between the sheep and the goats, between those who are blessed and those who are cursed—all these are based not on whether or not those being judged believe in Jesus, but rather on whether or not they have followed his commandment to feed the hungry, give water to the thirsty, welcome the stranger, clothe the naked, comfort the sick, visit the prisoner.

The kingdom of God is realized, and people are part of it, whenever and wherever people stand by each other, care for each other, and love God to the best of their ability, as they know God. The kingdom is realized whenever and wherever people love their neighbor as God has commanded and as God has loved us in giving his only Son that the world might be saved.

Some people, people like us, are called to know God as he has revealed himself in Jesus Christ, and to believe in Jesus, and to proclaim and embody and serve the kingdom of God as Jesus did. That is our Christian vocation—pure gift, immeasurable and unmerited gift of God—not something in which we can take pride, because we have done nothing to deserve it, as the Letter to the Ephesians reminded us today.

The words of today's Gospel reading are addressed to people who have received that call, that gift, that vocation, and who don't know what to do with it, who are hesitating. That is where Nicodemus finds himself. He is a member of the Jewish high council, the Sanhedrin. He comes to Jesus at night because he does not want to be seen. He comes to him as a great teacher to question him.

Nicodemus appears twice more in the Gospel of John. In John 7:50 he speaks up in the Sanhedrin to suggest that Jesus should not be condemned without being heard to determine the facts. In John 19:38–40, Nicodemus shows up with Joseph of Arimathea, described as "a disciple of Jesus, although a secret one for fear of the Jews," to give burial to Jesus. Nicodemus is never identified as a disciple of Jesus. We don't know if he ever accepted his vocation. In the context of the Gospel of John, Nicodemus stands for the people in the synagogue who were too timid to admit publicly that they believed in Jesus— an understandable fear at a time when to do so would have resulted in their being thrown out of the synagogue.

The words of today's Gospel are addressed to us who know and admire Jesus, who have been called to discipleship, who have been offered the gift of faith. Are we afraid to admit publicly that we believe in Jesus and that we have committed ourselves to follow his way? Is there enough evidence in our lives to convict us of being disciples of Jesus because of the way we live, or are we no different from those who do not believe? Are we believers only in the night, when there is no risk of being seen? Are we believers only in name, because to believe in Jesus in fact would call for difficult change, for costly conversion?

The way for a Christian to live is to follow Jesus and to imitate his example. The Johannine phrase for this is "doing the truth," or "acting in truth." It is not enough to believe or to speak the truth; we have to do it, to act on it, to live the truth of Jesus Christ. The Letter to the Ephesians speaks of "a life of good deeds which God prepared for us in advance" (2:10). This is how we become God's handiwork or, in another trans-lation, God's work of art. That is what we can become, if we let God do his work in us. It is not the result of the search for self-fulfillment or an attitude of self-sufficiency or of partici-pating in the human potential movement. It is a gift, it is grace, and, as Lent continues to remind us, it involves the cross.

God has so loved us that he has called us to know his Son, to believe in him, and to follow him, taking up our cross. Will we accept his call?

Prayer Is Not Enough

TIME: MARCH 28, 1982
SEASON: FIFTH SUNDAY OF LENT
SCRIPTURE READINGS: JEREMIAH 31:31–34; HEBREWS 5:7–9;
    JOHN 12:20–33

Both the Gospel reading and the second reading have implicit references to the agony of Jesus in the garden. The Gospel of John eliminates all incidents in the life of Jesus that may seem to imply weakness, but it usually retains the language of these events as we find them in the other Gospels. Today we hear: "My soul is troubled now, yet what should I say—Father save me from this hour? But it was for this that I came to this hour. Father glorify your name." I am sure you can hear the echo of the Synoptic Gospels' description of the struggle of Jesus in accepting the cup of suffering and the will of the Father.

In the reading from the Letter to the Hebrews we hear: "In the days when Christ was in the flesh, he offered prayers and supplications with loud cries and silent tears to God, who was able to save him from death, and he was heard because of his reverence" (5:7). He was heard, not by being spared suffering and death, but he was saved through death in the new life of resurrection.

The agony in the garden was probably for Jesus the most painful time, the deepest anguish, the complete surrender of his life into death, the moment of acceptance of death's unknown. Jesus asked for the support, the presence, the prayer of his friends to sustain him. He longed for human comfort—a touch, a word, a look that would express the love and care of those who were close to him. But they were asleep. Jesus needed them, and they missed their chance. How much did they miss when they failed to share that precious time with Jesus?

The last of the five points we have been developing during this Lenten season as the essential dimensions of our radical conversion is described by Father John Kavanaugh, S.J., as "openness to the poor; tithing of our time for those whom the culture deems expendable, unwanted, unproductive." But the startling part of his statement is that we should give our time to those who need us most not for their sake, but for our sake, for what we can learn, for what we can be given by the poor and those rejected by society: the severely handicapped, the brain damaged, the terminally ill, the prisoners, the very sick or very old, all who are distressed in any serious way.

This is not working for justice, to improve their situation, to assure their human dignity. This is for ourselves, for our nourishment and growth, for what we gain from the personal contact and relationship with those in pain or disabled. We are afraid of marginal people, handicapped people, people with severe illness, because we often do not know what to do with them. We are not in control of the situation. We are afraid to let go, to be faced with what we do not know how to handle. If we overcome that fear, if we make ourselves available, if we are willing to try to establish a truly mutual relationships, we will be enriched, changed.

St. Vincent de Paul said that the poor are everything we must become. We need to learn from them. Mother Teresa asked: Who ministers to whom? The poor give us so much if we allow ourselves to be ministered to. Father Kavanaugh uses two powerful examples: his mother going to help a woman totally incapacitated, and the story of himself and fellow Jesuits going to visit another Jesuit rendered helpless by successive strokes. I remember an old Italian woman to whom I used to take communion at home when I was a young priest. She was illiterate, but one of the wisest people I have ever known. I will never forget her outlook on life, her insight into what is truly real, what matters in the end, her clear, simple, sure, warm faith.

I know from my experience of caring for terminally ill people the love they have given me in return, how they have affirmed me in my ministry to them, made me feel useful, good, worthwhile—not only in celebrating the mystery of salvation that I tried to bring to them, but in what I am as a person. I hear people talk about their experience with street people: the warmth of their gratitude, the realization of their innate human dignity, the trust they put in those who share food with them. There is not much room for pretending, for phoniness, for playing games in these situations. We come to know ourselves as we really are. We have to come face to face with the reality of our own mortality and frailty and the possibility of becoming the one in need.

This tithing of our time to people in need for our own sake completes the picture of the Christian life that we have been trying to develop during this Lenten season. Prayer is not enough. It can be empty, isolated, self-centered. Working for justice cannot work without prayer or simplicity of life or openness to the poor. The ideological struggle, activity without reflection, doing without compassion, can be simply another way of seeking power. Community life cannot long be sustained without prayer and commitment to justice.

Nourished in prayer, letting God claim our whole life, surrendering our weakness to him so that we may be filled with his power, we go forth into our life, into our culture with all its temptations, and we try to establish personal relationships in the model of our loving covenant with God. We want God's covenant to embrace all human beings in justice and in peace, and we work to build a world where this is possible. We are willing to reduce our wants and live a simpler life, and we give time to the personal needs of others so that we may learn and be enriched by what the poor and the suffering and the unwanted and the unproductive have to give us.

Look at the pattern of Jesus' life. He begins his active life with baptism at the Jordan, where his covenant relationship with the Father is revealed: He is the beloved Son sent by the Father to be the presence of his love in the world. He is led into the desert, to solitude and prayer, and there he is tempted to power and property and pleasure and comfort. He is able to resist and to turn temptation into an affirmation of his fidelity to God, radically grounded in his abandonment to the Father. His life is unalterably changed. He becomes as one who has nothing, who is totally dependent on others for his material life. He becomes a person for others, and this is now his style of life.

Jesus returns from the desert filled with the Spirit and proclaims in the synagogue of Nazareth that he has been anointed to announce Good News to the poor, God's kingdom of liberty and justice and peace. He is in constant contact with the sick and the outcasts and the sinners and ministers to them, giving his time to the poor, healing them, attending to those in need. Finally, again, after a night of prayer, he begins to call companions to himself, to build a community to share his life, his mission, his destiny.

This is the meaning of life as we find it in Jesus Christ. This is the life to which we have been called through our baptism. This is the life that calls for our continuing, life-long conversion to deeper prayer and contemplation, to faithful covenants and intimacy, to justice and simplicity of life, to openness to the poor and the needs of others. This is the Christ-life.

Transformed by His Life

TIME: MARCH 31, 1994

SEASON: HOLY THURSDAY

SCRIPTURE READINGS: EXODUS 12:1–8, 11–14;
1 CORINTHIANS 11:23–26; JOHN 13:1–15

On a night not like any other night, in "a large upstairs room, furnished and ready" (Mark 14:15), Jesus gathered with his disciples to celebrate the Passover meal. This was a sacred and holy meal, filled with the chanting of psalms, the reading of the Scriptures, the sharing of ritual foods, all heavy with memories and meaning: the lamb sacrificed whose blood on the doorpost protected the Hebrews, the cup of deliverance drunk four times for the four promises of freedom in the book of Exodus, green herbs for the beauty of nature, salt water for the tears of the slaves and the passage through the Sea of Reeds, and more.

For Jesus and his disciples, the Passover meal was the joyous celebration of the freedom from slavery God had given their ancestors, a freedom renewed for every generation—however limited and precarious their present freedom—and the anticipation of the future fullness of freedom, in God's ultimate rescue of his people and of his creation. It was a time of spirited joy and excitement, of remembrance and hope.

Were the disciples aware of what was about to take place? Most likely they were not, but even as they were celebrating the historical passage from slavery to freedom, the disciples were about to witness the most dramatic changes in their own life.

When it came time for Jesus to break the matzo and show it to the others, he added something totally new and unexpected: "Take this and eat: this is my body, which I will give for you." And when it came time to drink of the third cup, Jesus took the cup, blessed it, and shared it, saying: "Take this and drink from it all of you: this is my blood of the new covenant, which is poured out for many." For a Jew like Jesus these words had a very precise meaning. Body, flesh, meant the human being, for that is what we are, this body, this flesh. Blood meant the very life of that body. What Jesus is saying is: This is the gift I give you, my whole self, my own very life. I am giving myself and my whole life to you and for you. Take it, make it your own. And Jesus said: "Do this in remembrance of me."

We are continents and centuries away from that room, and we are gathered here to do what Jesus asked us to do in remembrance of him. The world has changed in ways that no one in the first century could have envisioned. Even Jesus, in his human reality, could not foresee the kind of world in which we live, the kind of people we are, so different from the Palestinian Jews and Galilean peasants who were gathered with him on that holy night, so different even among ourselves—in our origins and background, in our thinking and feelings, in our lifestyles and dreams.

How the world has changed, even in our own memory! This is not the way we celebrated Holy Thursday when I was nineteen. How we have changed, in the way we understand and experience and celebrate the meaning of Jesus in the Eucharist! And yet we believe that the fundamental reality has not changed, that our celebration tonight renews the memory of the Lord's supper and makes it present to us once again.

Again for us now, as on that holy night, wheat that has been transformed into bread will become the Body of Christ. The grape that has been crushed into wine is about to become the Blood of Christ. And we, who have heard his call and have gathered to remember him and to do what he has asked us to do, are about to become one in him, to be changed into his body, a living organism animated by his spirit, sharing in his very life.

In one of the accounts of the Last Supper there is a haunting phrase that speaks of the intensity of Jesus' desire to do what he did: *"Desiderio desideravi:* With desire I have desired to eat this paschal meal with you." It tells me how deeply, how strongly, Jesus wanted to be with his friends, how much he wanted to be remembered, and to continue to be with them, even as death was about to separate them. With desire Jesus wants to share this meal with us tonight. We are here to remember him, and he is present in our midst.

Traditionally the Church has tried to describe the real presence of Jesus in the Eucharist as a "change in substance," *transubstantiation*. But modern science suggests that there is no substance lying at the heart of matter, only energy, a continuous transformation of energy, a new form of power hidden at the core of the sub-atomic particles of bread and wine, the very bodily and spiritual energy of the Risen Christ, the very power of God in Jesus Christ active at the heart of the matter.

Note the four actions of Jesus over the bread and the wine. He *took, blessed, broke,* and *gave.* As Jesus *took* the bread and the cup, so may he take us into his hands. He did not take the precious and the fancy, the rare and the singular. He took the common and the ordinary and made it his own. May he take us and hold each of us in his hands, and by his touch make us precious and unique, truly his own, ready to be transformed into the signs of his loving presence.

As Jesus *blessed* the bread and the cup and made them holy and sacred, set aside for God's service, filled with God's blessing and grace, so may we be blessed by Jesus' word and by his touch, and feel his call and empowerment to holiness. May we be willing to be consecrated for his service, to become his sacrament, always conscious that we carry with us his blessing and his gift of love-filled grace.

As Jesus *broke* the bread and shared the cup, we come to him with all our brokenness to be made whole, yet ready to be broken again, because it is only by being broken that the bread can be shared, only by being passed from hand to hand that the cup can become for everyone a sharing in Jesus' new life.

As Jesus *gave* the bread and wine to his disciples, blessed and broken and shared, he will give himself again to us this night, his whole self and his whole life, blessed and broken and shared, for our sake and for the sake of the world. And he wants us, his living body, to give ourselves to one another and to the world, to offer our life as part of the new covenant begun in him and to be completed in the fullness of God's kingdom.

May his life-saving, life-giving, death-conquering energy transform not only the bread and the wine but also each and every one of us, and our whole community, into the living sacraments of his presence, into the energy of his self-giving love.

Who Is This Jesus?

TIME: APRIL 3, 1994

SEASON: EASTER SUNDAY

SCRIPTURE READINGS: ACTS 10:34A, 37–43; COLOSSIANS 3:1–4;
    JOHN 20:1–9

If you have been reading the religion pages in newspapers and magazines in recent months, you have become aware of a number of new books that question in a radical way the identity of Jesus. The one most widely discussed is *Jesus: A Revolutionary Biography* by the biblical scholar Dominic Crossan, one of the leaders of the "Jesus Seminar." I have not read the book, but, according to the reviews, it presents Jesus as an illiterate, low-caste artisan who hardly said ten percent of the words attributed to him, did not cure anyone, advocated a radical egalitarianism that got him into trouble, and was killed by the Romans as a dangerous subversive. There was no resurrection. His corpse, like that of all abandoned criminals, went into a shallow grave, vulnerable to the wild dogs that roamed the wasteland of the execution grounds.[18]

I am waiting to receive the massive new work of Raymond Brown, *The Death of the Messiah*. I very much like the way someone has differentiated Brown's research and conclusions from those of Crossan. Brown says that his research has convinced him that the Gospels are 80 percent reliable memories of historical events and 20 percent the product of the faith of the disciples. For Crossan, 80 percent is pure fiction and retrospective myth-making on the part of writers who had "already decided on the transcendental importance of the adult Jesus,"[19] and only 20 percent is memory with a historical kernel.

I find myself standing solidly with Raymond Brown, because I have tremendous respect for his work, which I find immensely illuminating and always firmly supportive of my faith understanding and experience. Crossan's work impresses me as being very largely guesswork, and a new form of myth-making based on the scientific myths that have become the modern dogmas, especially in the social sciences.

I do not bring up these references to engage in scholarly debate, but to ask why the views of Crossan, of the "Jesus

Seminar," and of others attempting to deconstruct the Christian Scriptures, seem to be so immediately popular. I believe it is because our culture is not very comfortable with a Jesus who speaks and acts with the authority of the fullness of God abiding in him. Our world seems much more comfortable with Jesus as an ordinary man, with revolutionary charisma and courageous leadership qualities, whom we can admire as a good teacher and model of "authentic" human life. To see Jesus in this light makes it much easier to pick and choose the teachings we want to accept and those which, in our estimation, no longer speak to the modern mind.

If we accept this revised understanding of Jesus, we can continue to judge what is of value in our life by a personal "feel good" index. We can reduce Jesus to the level of our own humanity and ignore the intrusion of the divine demand of mutual love and compassion into our history. This reductionist view of Jesus can even be made to justify our self-seeking individualism and allow us to continue living as we please, without facing the risk of change and transformation in our life and in our culture.

In this view of Jesus we come to the Easter liturgy as to an annual spring festival, a celebration of the cycle of life and death that nature renews for us every year. But that is not the Jesus of the Gospels or the Jesus of our experience of faith. The Jesus of the Gospels lived and taught and acted out of the fullness of the power of God abiding in him. The Jesus of the Gospels died on the cross for our sins and was raised from death by the power of God for our salvation.

If we are gathered here as his disciples, we must be willing to share both the faith and the stories of the first followers of Jesus. We share with them the puzzlement, the doubt, and the uncertainty as we stand before the empty tomb. But through their eyes, and through their faith, we also come to see and believe. And what we believe is what Peter preaches as he speaks to the household of Cornelius, the first Gentile to be caught up in this new movement of faith.

We believe that Jesus was anointed with the Spirit and the power of God, that he went about doing good, healing and setting free, and that the power of God was evident in him. The authorities killed him by hanging him on a tree, but God raised him up on the third day, and Peter insists that he has seen him and shared a meal with him in his risen life. Paul tells us that by baptism we also have died with Christ and now share his new life.

We do not have all the pieces of the puzzle, we cannot say that we understand all that the stories are trying to tell us. We know that the stories have come not only from the memory of the first witnesses but also from their experience of faith in Jesus and their expectation of his return. But we trust that they tell us the truth about Jesus' death and resurrection, for we ourselves have experienced the presence of the risen, living Jesus in our midst, and the power of his grace, especially in the breaking of the bread. We believe that Jesus lives—in our hearts, in our community gathered in his name, in the sacramental signs of his loving presence.

If we believe in the saving death and resurrection of Jesus, we know that we can't enter a new life without shedding the old, we can't share in the triumph of Jesus without sharing his struggle. If we are looking for communion in the resurrection of Jesus without sharing in his suffering and death, we will discover that our Easter will be over and forgotten within the week.

Easter cannot be just a yearly event for us, just a beautiful spring festival. We must let the transforming power of the Risen Christ touch every aspect of our life. Easter must change us, make us different, make us new. We must be like newborn babies, filled with new life, eager to grow into its fullness, so that when Christ, our life, appears, we may appear with him in glory (Col. 3:4).

Meeting the Risen Christ

TIME: APRIL 14, 1985

SEASON: SECOND SUNDAY OF EASTER

SCRIPTURE READINGS: ACTS 4:32–25; 1 JOHN 5:1–6;
  JOHN 20:19–31

Poor Thomas. For two thousand years, and perhaps for thousands more, he has been known and will continue to be known as "doubting Thomas." He is like someone from Missouri, the "Show Me" state, someone who demands to be shown, who always needs concrete, tangible proof for everything he hears.

There is nothing wrong with doubt. Hillaire Belloc said: "There falls no shadow where there shines no sun," and P.J. Bailey stated: "Where doubt, there truth is—'tis her shadow." There is a healthy skepticism that asks for more than hearsay and rumors when it comes to matters of supreme importance.

Try to hear Thomas express his feelings to the other disciples. "What you are saying is too awesome, too impossible, too incredible. It shatters our way of thinking and seeing things. I can't accept it just on your word. Somehow I must experience it myself. Somehow the Risen Jesus must touch me personally, so that I may come to my own faith response. Otherwise, it is only your faith that I accept."

I believe that this kind of attitude finds a parallel in our own life. In a sense, our faith is rooted in the resurrection faith and witness of those who saw and believed. Without that, nothing would have come down to us. We also begin by accepting the faith of others—parents, teachers, church, friends, models. In this way, we begin without seeing.

But is this enough? I don't believe so. In some way we need to meet the Risen Christ ourselves. In some way we need to come to our own personal faith in the resurrection. In some way we need to feel the presence of the Risen Christ in our life, calling us by name, giving us peace, sending us forth.

I believe that this is part of the attraction of the more fundamentalist, evangelical, charismatic churches. They seem to have a way of leading people to a powerful, emotional, intensely personal experience of Christ and of the Spirit. But that is not the only way to know the power of the Risen Christ in one's life. Not everyone is attracted to or moved by or able to accept the born-again experience. And the Gospel narratives of the resurrection make it very clear that even the first disciples came to faith, came to know the Risen Christ and the power of his new life in them, in different ways.

Can you think of times when this has happened to you? Can you name in your own life the experience of dying and rising with Christ, the experience of faith in his saving power and new life in his Spirit? Paul was brought to his knees and blinded, and needed another disciple to touch him. Mary Magdalen thought she had lost the Lord. Peter was asked three times: "Do you love me?" The two disciples on the road to Emmaus first felt something in their hearts as the stranger was explaining the Scriptures, and finally recognized the Risen Lord in the breaking of the bread. Some disciples encountered the risen Lord and the gift of the Spirit as a community gathered in prayer. Peter and John know the power of Christ at work in them when they cure the lame man on their way to the temple to pray.

For me, the most powerful and moving experiences have been in liturgical celebrations; in feelings of overwhelming beauty and harmony, such as listening to Bach's *St. Matthew Passion;* in a personal encounter with another person, the faith of an old woman who is dying, being able to help someone pass from death to life; in tears, both of sadness and of joy.

What are the signs, how do we recognize these moments of faith? God is part of the moment. We are brought to think of Jesus; we become aware of his presence. There is peace and joy, even in the midst of loss, mourning, suffering, hurt, injustice. There is a new desire to live a life of love and service, the kind of life described in the reading from Acts.

We are able to say: "My Lord and my God!" The words are not important. The important thing is: the sense that there is a transcendent mystery that cares for me, a power greater than I am, greater than all history and human endeavor, greater than all the forces of creation, and that this mystery, this power, is gracious; a sense of purpose, direction, wholeness to my life and to all there is; a sense of trust in a goodness greater than I can understand; the willingness to let the Lord rule my life and direct it; the decision to let go of the control of myself and others and to put control where it belongs, in God's power.

My Lord and my God!

At Heaven's Gate?

TIME: APRIL 13, 1997

SEASON: THIRD SUNDAY OF EASTER

SCRIPTURE READINGS: ACTS 3:13–15, 17–19; 1 JOHN 2:1–5A;
      LUKE 24:35–48

In the past couple of weeks I have been reading a number of stories about the mass suicide of thirty-nine people in a mansion in Rancho Santa Fe. I keep hoping to discover a better answer to explain what happened, a better theory to try to make sense of what seems to me to be such a disturbing, senseless, irrational decision and choice. I did not find any good explanations and probably never will.

What I found is that almost all the writers try to compare Heaven's Gate with other religious experiences, especially with Christian faith, with Christian belief in the resurrection and the survival of the human person after death, with the Christian hope of a new life as a sharing of the resurrection of Jesus and the hope of heaven, and a belief in the ultimate transformation of our world, the coming of new heavens and a new earth.

One writer even compared the thirty-nine people who killed themselves at Rancho Santa Fe with the martyrs who were killed because they refused to deny their faith in Jesus and to sacrifice to idols and to the image of the Roman emperor. I find this kind of comparison very troubling, very distorted, very damaging.[20]

It is possible to take statements from some Christian groups on the margins of the main Christian traditions and make them sound very much like some of the statements we have read or heard on television coming from the members of Heaven's Gate. It is also possible to take phrases and images from traditional Christianity, quote them out of context, and make them sound like the language of some esoteric cult.

Some of the authentic doctrines of Christianity, from the Bible and the ancient, valid traditions of the historical Church, can be presented in an abstract, theoretical fashion, analyzed using the scientific method and the test of scientific evidence, resulting in the suggestion that there is not much difference between the beliefs of members of Heaven's Gate and believing Christians.

It might be helpful for us to reflect on some of the radical differences between a cult, such as Heaven's Gate, and the Christian religion, Christian faith, and a Christian community.

The first important difference is the two-thousand-year history of the Church. A cult, especially one of the more extreme, may last for a number of years but then gradually, or—as in the case of Heaven's Gate—suddenly, disappear. A cult's life is often dependent on a strong, persuasive, hypnotic leader. When that leader dies, the followers soon disperse and the group disintegrates.

In the case of Christianity, it is precisely after its leader died, after Jesus was crucified, and after he was experienced as still present among his small, original group of followers as the Risen Lord, that the movement began to grow. I have no doubt that the movement of the believers of Jesus looked like a cult to the leaders of the established Jewish synagogues, but it survived conflicts and persecutions and continued to grow.

Throughout the two thousand years of Christianity, other groups have formed and separated from the mainstream. At first they were regarded as sects or cults, but some of them have survived and are now accepted as variant forms of the Judeo-Christian faith. Even more striking is the fact that Christianity survived not only the many divisions and separations, but also the internal corruption, immorality, ambition, greed, and power struggles—at times quite rampant—from top to bottom in the Church. Only God's providential care for his Church has enabled it to survive and thrive.

A second fundamental difference between the martyrs and the suicides at Rancho Santa Fe is that the martyrs did not kill themselves, which might have been an attractive way to avoid the cruelty of their persecutors. They were willing to suffer torture and even death because they chose to remain faithful to Christ. At times we do find the extravagant language of some saint about a desire for martyrdom, and some no doubt attempted to seek it, but the majority of the martyrs were simple, ordinary people who made the choice to serve God rather than the earthly powers that threatened their life.

Third, it seems to me that the ultimate test of the truth of a belief, of a religious commitment, of the validity and goodness of a movement, is the one suggested by Jesus in the Gospels: "By their fruits you will know them!" What kind of results does this faith, this commitment, bring forth in the life of those who believe, those who follow the movement?

This became very clear to me this past week, when I read a couple of articles on Cardinal Joseph Bernardin, the Archbishop of Chicago who died last fall. I was deeply struck and affected by the obvious contrasts between his life and death and what the media were revealing about Heaven's Gate. I will not draw out the contrasts. I will simply mention three aspects of Cardinal Bernardin's legacy that vividly brought home to me the differences between a lived experience of Christian faith and a cult.

The first difference is in Cardinal Bernardin's attitude toward death. He was able to embrace death as a friend who would lead him home to God. He was able to articulate his profoundly spiritual understanding of death during the last months of his life. There seemed to be no resentment, no fear or anxiety in him. But his friends have also made very clear that Cardinal Bernardin experienced the universal fear and anxiety about death that we all face, the fear of death experienced as loss and brokenness and the inevitable limit to our human reality. He publicly acknowledged that he needed help in facing the reality of death, in coming to understand death as a friend. We know that for the first time in his life he wept uncontrollably. He did know anger and fear in the face of death.

Second, Cardinal Bernardin did not isolate himself, but made use of his illness to reach out to other persons who like him were facing the threat of death because of cancer, persons whom he met in doctors' offices, in hospitals, and in cancer centers. He reached out to them, shared his agony and their agony, and was able to give them courage and hope, to be for them the sign of the loving presence of God, the instrument of God's compassionate love.

Third, after he was diagnosed with terminal cancer, Cardinal Bernardin did not turn his back on the world or try to escape it or regard it as an accumulation of evil from which he sought to be free. On the contrary, he continued until the very end, as long as he had any strength left, to give of himself for the good of others, to try to make the world a better place. He continued to lead the Archdiocese of Chicago in its spiritual journey, to promote the Common Ground Initiative—an attempt to overcome the divisions in the Church. He continued his courageous witness to his consistent ethic of life by writing letters to the Supreme Court against physician-assisted suicide and to the president to support the ban on partial birth abortion.

Are these also the fruits that our Christian faith produces in our lives?

> The ability to face adversity with courage, to recognize the darkness that is part of our human condition, but also to know the power of God to overcome evil with goodness and darkness with light, to bring forth a new creation for ourselves individually, for our communities, for our world;

> the willingness to share our journey of suffering and pain, as well as joy and peace, with one another, to sustain one another on our journey toward death and new life, to stand by each other when we need one another;

> the courage to dedicate ourselves to changing our world, to work for the gospel values proclaimed by Jesus, to work for justice and peace for all our brothers and sisters.

Today's second reading, from the First Letter of John, insists that to really know the mystery of Christ, to make sure that the love of God is made perfect in us, we must keep Jesus' word, Jesus' commandments. In the Gospel of John, which reflects the same tradition as the letter, there is only one commandment: We are to love one another as Jesus has loved us, the Jesus who said: "Greater love than this no one has, than to lay down one's life for one's friends." By these fruits we will recognize true faith and authentic religious experience.

A friend gave me a copy of an Easter creed that was used in another church. I would like to use it as our Easter affirmation of faith today:

We believe in an Easter God who transforms darkness into light, hatred into tolerance, despair into hope.

We believe God is always working for good, changing every Friday nightmare into an Easter dream of new possibility.

We believe in the Risen Christ, who befriends us on our roads of searching and worry; who touches us through song and silence, word and gesture; who calls us by name to enter the dance of life.

We believe in the Spirit, the hidden presence behind every resurrection, who beckons us to leave the safety of the tomb and trust in the gracious invitation to live joyfully.

We believe the Spirit is always renewing the church and making us a people who practice kindness, encourage beauty, and work for justice and freedom.

We believe we are an Easter people, a sign that with God all things are possible.

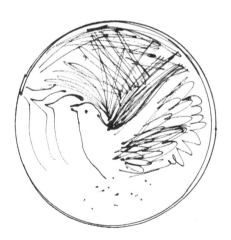

Who Will Be Our Shepherd?

TIME: APRIL 24, 1994
SEASON: FOURTH SUNDAY OF EASTER
SCRIPTURE READINGS: ACTS 4:8–12; 1 JOHN 3:1–2; JOHN 10:11–18

It is not often now that we see shepherds at their work in the fields, and therefore we may find it difficult to grasp the meaning of the beautiful imagery of Jesus as the good shepherd. This week I came across a description of a school crossing guard, and it made me think that perhaps this familiar sight can serve as a modern counterpart to the image of the good shepherd.

Try to imagine this scene. It is mid-afternoon and the crossing guard waits for the children at the busy intersection as she has done for years. The children approach the corner running and yelling, oblivious to all the cars that go rushing by. But they stop right next to the crossing guard. She is a familiar and expected presence, and their trust in her is implicit and complete. The woman greets the children warmly, and she knows each one of them by name. She watches the traffic until it is safe to lead them across. She moves to the middle of the street and stands there until the cars stop. Then she calls to the children and they cross under her protective watch. She talks to the children as they go by, and waits until each one has crossed safely. And then she returns to the corner, to wait for other children who depend on her for their safe passage. [21]

I hope this image helps us understand some of the qualities of the biblical image of the good shepherd: warm affection and tender care, intimate knowledge and relationship, careful protection and guidance, the willingness to take risks for those entrusted to one's care. That is the way Jesus, our good shepherd, is with us. That is why there is safety and comfort, freedom and abandon, trust in the knowledge that Jesus sees himself in that kind of relationship with us.

But there is more to the biblical metaphor of the shepherd. In the texts we often find a contrast between good and bad shepherds, between the good shepherd and the hired hand, as heard in today's Gospel. The bad shepherds, the hired hands, are often the leaders of God's people who are found wanting in the discharge of the responsibilities that God has entrusted to them. In biblical language the shepherd is an image for a leader of the people.

What are the qualities of this biblical leadership? The texts that use the imagery of the shepherd speak of responsible care, guiding in the right path, providing protection and safety, comfort and nurture, with a disposition of goodness and mercy. Good shepherding, good leadership, in the model of Jesus, is knowing, free, and faithful. First of all, we need to know each other and be known. Our world is becoming more and more impersonal. Our communication technologies, for all their marvels, allow and encourage us to be distant from one another, to avoid face-to-face encounter. The leader is challenged to know each one by name—even more, by heart—and to respond with care that is motivated by knowledge and love.

Second, our care must be given freely. As a leader I am called to serve, not out of a sense of obligation, because I have to, but out of a genuine desire to serve, because I choose to serve. A leader in the image of Jesus, the good shepherd, is one who is able to make the people whom he serves feel that they are making a gift to him or to her, offering an opportunity, not imposing a burden.

Third, the leader must remain faithful even in the face of rejection, even in the experience of being powerless to help or take away the pain. It is this presence, knowing that the good shepherd is by our side, that gives us the courage to walk through the valley of darkness and death.

That darkness has many names today: unemployment, homelessness, addiction, broken relationships, worries for the future of our children, fear of violence, loss and loneliness, failing health, painful transitions. We cannot resolve all these problems or take away all the pain, but we must be able to stand by each other and take away the fear of evil by the assurance that the power of all this pain cannot overcome the power of the risen Jesus. It is his presence that we must make real by our shepherding.

Today we are asked to pray for priestly vocations. We are all well aware of the critical scarcity of ordained ministers. The latest issue of our diocesan publication informs us that in two areas nearby parishes have been joined together with one ordained priest serving two or three communities. Will prayer solve the crisis? No, it will not. I certainly do not mean to minimize the role and the importance of prayer in this and in all matters. But I am also convinced that we have to look at the situation realistically and be willing to make whatever changes are necessary. The Church needs to reconsider the way it looks at ministry, especially ordained priesthood, and reflect on who may be called to ordained ministry today.

I have heard reports about a talk given by Archbishop Quinn of San Francisco at a convention of the National Catholic Education Association, which apparently contained some important observations. Unfortunately, I have not seen the text or even news stories, so I am going only on hearsay. First, Archbishop Quinn suggested that we cannot expect the seminaries to do the impossible. Out of a society full of young people who have experienced all kinds of brokenness, who have been wounded, who have not had the opportunity to reach an adequate level of maturity, we cannot expect the candidates for priestly ordination to be any different from the rest of society. The Church has to be willing and prepared to deal with the situation as it is.

Second, Archbishop Quinn asks: Where should the Church be looking for healthy, whole, mature leadership today? I am not sure of his answer, but I suspect that we are not going to find that kind of leadership among 18- to 24-year-old single males. We need to look for people who have been able to go beyond their woundedness and brokenness, who have gone through the struggle and the pain and have survived, who have overcome dysfunctions and reached a level of stability, maturity, wisdom, and spiritual depth that will enable them to help others, to be good shepherds to the broken and the wounded.

Where will the Church find this kind of person? Probably among older people, and they will not all be single, and they will not all be male. If we are serious about encouraging the best possible people for the ordained priesthood, I am convinced that the Church needs to rethink the question of who will be an acceptable candidate for ordination. Whom is God really calling to ordained priestly ministry in our day?

Ordained ministry is not the only ministry in the Church today. All of you are called to some form of ministry. All of you are called to be shepherds to God's holy people, in one way or another. It may be for only one person, or two, or it may be for a family, for a classroom, for an office. The good shepherd has gathered us for this time of worship, and has revealed to us again how he cares for us knowingly, freely, faithfully. Now he will send us forth to care for one another, even as he has cared for us.

Grafted onto the True Vine

TIME: MAY 5, 1985

SEASON: FIFTH SUNDAY OF EASTER

SCRIPTURE READINGS:: ACTS 9:26–31; 1 JOHN 3:18–24;
JOHN 15:1–8

In all of literature it would be difficult to find a more direct and forceful use of the metaphor than in the Gospel of John. A metaphor is a figure of speech that makes a comparison by a direct statement, without using words such as "like" and "as." In the fourth Gospel, Jesus *is* the Lamb of God, the bread of life, the light of the world.

In theology, the metaphor, or the use of analogy, is the only way we have to speak about God, about the mystery of reality that cannot be captured or contained in our ordinary speech and language. The metaphor helps us to enter that mystery, to begin to understand or feel the meaning of God for us, and our connection with him.

Today's Gospel, taken from the long speech of Jesus at the last supper, has a striking, marvelous metaphor: Jesus is the vine, we are the branches. The metaphor of the vine has a long tradition in the history of salvation and in biblical literature. In Isaiah 5:1–7, the "song of the vineyard" describes Israel, God's people, and their relationship to Yahweh. Psalm 80 pleads with God to take care of his vineyard, his vine, which has been trampled and practically destroyed. Hosea 14:5–8 promises that Israel will one day again "bloom like the vine" and that God will love her freely.

This is the vine that speaks when Jesus utters his words. Now he is the true vine, the real vine, whom the Father has planted in the world and in history. He is the new Israel, in him is born the new people of God, obedient to the Father, responsive to his protective, tender, nurturing care.

There is another element in today's Gospel to which I need to call your attention: the words "I am." This is how God identifies himself to Moses when Moses asks for his name. This is the origin of the name Yahweh, God's proper name, so to speak, which became so sacred that the Jews did not say it and even forgot how to pronounce it. In the Gospel of John, whenever you see these words, it should be like a light turned on to warn you that it is the eternal Son of God speaking, the Word of God made flesh, the Risen Lord.

So today we hear the very mystery of God fully present in Jesus say to us: I am the true vine . . . you are the branches. What does that mean? What does it say to us? As I was reflecting and praying on this passage, the metaphor suddenly assumed tremendous power for me when I thought of it as the action of grafting.

It has been a long time since I have seen grafting done. I had to refresh my memory. You know that grafting is taking a budding stem of one variety of grapes, roses, peaches, what have you, and implanting it into another vine, or tree, or limb. There has to be a cut in the stock receiving the graft, and the other vine is put into the cut and bound tight. It begins to draw its sustenance, its very life, from the other. It becomes part of the other, although it retains its own identity and will continue to bear its own kind of fruit.

There has to be similarity and compatibility. God becomes human so that we can be grafted onto him. We draw our nurture, our very life, from him. Through baptism we are alive in his life. Each of us retains his or her personal individuality. All of us are empowered to bear fruit, according to that individual identity.

Jesus is the vine and we are the branches. He is our life energy. Is that true? Where do you go to be energized, to come alive? Psychologists say that the extroverted person needs other people, a crowd, a party, an event, and that the introverted person needs to be alone, to spend time in peace, quiet, silence to be renewed.

We Christians need to go to Christ to be energized. If we are extroverts, we may need a liturgical celebration, a prayer group, celebration or pastoral work with others. If we are introverts, we will need centering prayer, stillness and silence, meditation and contemplation. More accurately, we all need both kinds of experiences, encounters with the source of our life, with a different balance depending on our natural inclination.

Christ, the true vine, the real life, is here, and we are part of him. But we need to stay in him, to draw that life from him, to be energized by him—by his word, his sacraments, his presence, his nearness, his love—and we will bear much fruit. What is this fruit? How do we know if we live in him and he lives in us? I believe the answer begins with the words that opened the second reading: "Little children, let us love in deed and in truth and not merely talk about it. This is our way of knowing that we are committed to the truth and are at peace before him" (1 John 3:18).

Love Wins

Time: May 8, 1994
Season: Sixth Sunday of Easter (Mother's Day)
Scripture Readings: Acts 10:25–26, 34–35, 44–48;
     1 John 4:7–10; John 15:9–17

The whole Easter message can be summed up by saying that love wins. The love of the Father for the Son won the victory over death. The love of Jesus for his friends made him willing to lay down his life, and so to win the victory over sin for us. If we really loved one another as he has loved us, we would have the power to transform the world, to bring an end to violence and to establish peace, to overcome evil and to bring forth God's new creation in his risen Son.

There are people who think that all this emphasis on love is destroying our Church and our society. They blame the Second Vatican Council and "new age" thinking for this, and they want to go back to the time when we talked more about law and obligations, obedience and responsibility, and less about love. Love can be used to justify almost any kind of license and behavior, they say. We need clear-cut rules of conduct, we need to bring back appropriate rewards and punishments, and everything will be better again.

I am sure nobody in this community thinks along those lines. Am I right? But just in case you ever find yourself in a discussion with someone who thinks that love is the easy way out and the creation of a new liberal permissiveness in the Church, let's talk about love for a little while.

First of all, the idea that love is the defining experience of our relationship with God did not begin with Vatican II. You heard it in today's biblical texts. Jesus says: "As the Father has loved me, so I have loved you. Live on in my love. You will live in my love if you keep my commandments."

Ah! There are the commandments! Yes, Jesus says: "This is my commandment: Love one another as I have loved you." He insists: "The command I give you is this: that you love one another." There are a number of other passages in our Christian Scriptures that speak of love, and they are among the most beautiful in our tradition. Many are very well known, such as the famous hymn to love in 1 Corinthians 13. The point I want to make is that in biblical traditions the fundamental call and invitation, the first and greatest of all commandments, is to love God and to love one another.

Maybe the problem, then, is in our understanding of the meaning of love. Biblical love is not synonymous with license, and love is not the easy way out. Love is not just romantic feeling, physical attraction, emotional attachment. Love is choice and decision. Love is willful commitment and faithful service. Listen to Paul again: "Love is patient; love is not envious or boastful or arrogant or rude. It does not insist on its own way; it is not irritable or resentful; it does not rejoice in wrongdoings, but rejoices in truth. It bears all things, believes all things, hopes all things, endures all things" (1 Cor. 13: 4–7). I don't see anything very easy in that kind of love.

The story of Peter and Cornelius, suggested by the first reading, can also teach us something about love. It is one of the most important events in the history of the early Church, because Cornelius is the first Gentile to become a believer in Christ and a disciple. In the story, Peter has a strange vision: A large sheet full of animals, reptiles, and birds is lowered in front of him and a voice tells him, "Kill and eat." Peter is horrified. He eats only kosher food and keeps himself clean from all impure contacts. But the voice tells him: "What God has made clean you must not call profane." This is such a shocking message that the whole thing has to be repeated three times.

At that point messengers arrive from Cornelius to ask Peter to come with them to Caesarea. At the urging of the angel, Peter agrees to go. This is a very daring and courageous action on the part of Peter, because he is going against the laws and practices of his religious traditions. He is taking a great risk of ritual impurity by coming into contact with a Gentile and entering his house. Once Peter gets there and begins to tell the story of Jesus, he gains an extraordinary insight: God is not a racist or a religious bigot. God shows no partiality to anyone because of racial or ethnic or religious background. The Spirit of God fills the hearts of Cornelius and all his family even before Peter can decide whether or not they are ready to be baptized. Amazing, isn't it?

God's love does not pay any attention to our prejudices and narrow-mindedness! What do you think that means for us in reference to things that are happening in Haiti, in Rwanda, in Bosnia, even in Fresno? Do you still think that love is the easy way out when it means that we cannot keep our biases and hang on to our prejudices about whom we like or dislike, whom we are willing or unwilling to help, when we have to love even our enemies?

Today is Mother's Day, and a mother's love is a great example of what love means. I don't mean the commercial exploitation of romantic notions of motherly love. I mean the hard, day-to-day dedication of a mother to the well-being of her family, of her children, even when it means the sacrifice of her own self, the laying down of her own life, daily. I am not talking about a woman who has it all, but about a woman who does it all. So many mothers today hold down full-time jobs, have careers, and volunteer to help the larger community while also cooking, doing the laundry, finding socks, remembering birthdays, checking the homework, and getting up in the middle of the night to find the cough medicine. That's what love means. That is not all, but that is certainly part of it. We can think of our own mother and the many concrete ways she expressed her love for us and empowered us to love.

At its best a mother's love, like God's love, is truly unconditional, able to embrace and to love not only the perfect and the beautiful but also the broken and the handicapped, the physically or mentally impaired, the less than beautiful, the less than perfect. There is an intolerance of imperfection in our society that I find ominous. There are trends that seem to move in the direction of putting all kinds of conditions on the love for a child. If the child is healthy, perfect, intelligent, comes at a convenient time, is the desired sex, I will love you. Otherwise, I don't want you.[22]

When I think of this, I remember God's words in Isaiah: "Can a woman forget her nursing child, or show no compassion for the child of her womb? Even if these may forget, yet I will never forget you" (Isaiah 49:15). We can celebrate God's love as a mother's love, and this is the most important thing that I want to say about love today: not that we can love God, but that God has loved us first, has revealed his love for us, and has called us to share the very intimacy of the love of Father and Son and Spirit.

The most unheard of, radical, revolutionary statement in the Scriptures today is that Jesus, the Risen Lord, has called us friends, has called us to genuine friendship with him and with the Father in the Spirit. It is because God has loved us that we are able to love one another. It is because he has made us his friends, and called us into the intimacy of his life and love, that love has become the defining experience of our relationship with God and the one commandment that surpasses all others. We are to love one another as God has loved us.

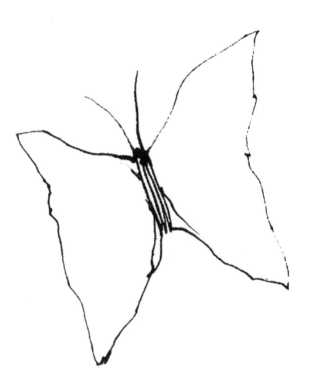

A Time for Parting

TIME: MAY 15, 1994 (NEWMAN CENTER 30ᵀᴴ ANNIVERSARY
AND FATHER NEGRO'S LAST SUNDAY AS PASTOR)
SEASON: ASCENSION OF THE LORD
SCRIPTURE READINGS: ACTS 1:1–11; EPHESIANS 4:1–13;
MARK 16:15–20

The disciples in today's story must have felt like a child who sees a cherished kite or a balloon soaring into the sky, irretrievably lost. When that string slips out of the tiny hand, the wrenching sense of loss evokes desperate tears. We have seen it happen here, on Palm Sunday, when the little children are asked to let go of their balloons to symbolize the change of mood from the triumphant entry of Jesus into Jerusalem, to the somber reading of the passion.

Imagine the agony and astonishment the disciples must have felt when Jesus was lifted up and disappeared into the cloud, as the story in Acts describes it. At that moment Jesus, who had become for them the essence of all their hopes and possibilities for the future, who made them feel powerful by his nearness, who had filled their hearts with joyous delight, left them with their eyes unable to see him and their imagination unable to grasp the meaning of what had happened.[23]

There is a contradiction in today's readings. The story in Acts speaks of Jesus leaving and being gone until his return in some distant future. The Gospel speaks of his continued presence and power at work in the disciples. The passages are talking about different kinds of presence, but we need to say more.

Luke's great insight of faith, recorded in Acts, divides the whole of salvation history into three great periods: the period of Israel, the period of Jesus—which is the very center of history, and the period of the Church, which begins at Pentecost. In Luke's vision, Jesus must leave so that the time of the Church may begin and the disciples may realize that now it is up to them to carry on the work of his salvation. The disciples must stop relying on Jesus to do it all and must get on with their task: to make salvation in Jesus Christ visible and concrete for their time in history, to be the witnesses to Jesus' words and deeds, death and resurrection to the very ends of the earth.

This is our feast day, because we are the Church, and this is our time. We live in Luke's great historical period of the Church, which extends until the day when Jesus will return in glory to establish the fullness of God's kingdom. The feast of the Ascension is our feast because it celebrates the fact that our humanity, in Jesus, became part of the mystery of God, and the promise that our own humanity is destined to be with Jesus in the glory of God.

We are the Church, all of us, charged with proclaiming the Good News of what God has done for us in Jesus Christ. We are to bear witness to Jesus, the fullness of God made flesh for our salvation, in our words and deeds, in our own life and death. But where are the signs that are to accompany our proc-lamation and the witness of our faith?

They are here, if we can only see them. For we are expel-ling our modern demons whenever we are able to overcome, whether in ourselves or in others, the demons of addiction, pride, and selfishness. We speak new languages whenever we open ourselves to new cultures and people different from us, when we learn to speak their language so that we can under-stand each other better. We are handling serpents, the ancient symbol of evil, whenever we are willing to take the risk to name and to confront the evils of our time. The poison of that evil will not harm us if we stay in touch with the Lord who is at work within us. And we bring God's healing power to others by our presence and words and touch, by a genuine concern for all who are sick and who suffer.

My dear friends, do you know what Jesus Christ is doing at the right hand of the Father? He is waiting for us, until all his enemies are overcome (Hebrews 10:13). We often piously think that we are waiting for Jesus, when in fact he is waiting for us to do our job here on earth, to help him overcome his enemies and to build the kingdom.

One commentary I read this past week suggested that for the disciples the Ascension of Jesus was like the emotional experience of losing someone important in our life, someone who has mediated for us a deeper access to the divine, through loving acceptance, creative energy, insights of wisdom, challenges to integrity and commitment.[24]

I think I know what was in the hearts of the disciples. This is the way I feel this morning. If I have mediated for you the mysteries of God's grace, you have been the channels of God's presence and blessing for me. You have embodied God's loving acceptance, creative energy, wisdom in faith, and challenges in love for me. This community has incredible talents, creativity, and energy. There is tremendous power in you, and I thank God for all the many ways you have put this power to work in the service of God and our brothers and sisters. I will miss you very much.

There are two things I want to say for myself today. First, one of my greatest fears has always been that I might use the gifts that God has given me for my own advantage, that my ministry would become a personal following rather than a journey together in the following of Jesus.

I hope that you have been able to receive my ministry as the power of God working through me. If I have led you to the Lord, and many of you have told me that I have been an instrument in your discovery of deeper faith and love of God, then I leave with complete confidence, because his presence will continue here in your midst, without change or interruption. Jesus Christ, our Lord and Savior, continues to be fully alive in your hearts and in this community. I entrust you all to his loving care.

The second thing I want to say is this. Since I announced that I would be leaving the Newman Center, I have been overwhelmed by all that many of you have said and written to me, to tell me the ways in which I have touched you and made a difference in your life. When I mentioned this to my spiritual director, he told me, very simply: "Give thanks to God with all your heart for having worked so many of his wonderful graces and blessings through you." I am humbled, and grateful to God with all my heart, and grateful to you for the way you have supported my ministry and myself personally.

There is a wonderful story, titled *Dragon Kite of the Autumn Moon*, that shows how the release of healing energy often depends on the capacity of the heart to let go of the most beloved treasure.[25] It is the story of a boy, Tad-Tin, and his beloved grandfather, set in the context of the Taiwanese celebration of Kite Day. The tradition is that every kite is set free at the end of the day so that it can carry away all the troubles.

This Kite Day the grandfather was too ill to make a kite for Tad-Tin and himself to fly together, as they had always done. If Tad-Tin were to participate in Kite Day he would have to fly the magnificent dragon kite the grandfather had made to celebrate Tad-Tin's birth. Finally he decided to do it, but his heart ached at the thought of losing the splendid dragon.

At the end of the day, his face wet with tears, he let go of the string and the kite soared away. When he returned home, he discovered that his grandfather had miraculously been restored to health. The story, and our passage from Ascension to Pentecost, tell us that sometimes we must let go of our most treasured possessions in order for them to be returned to us. "If I do not leave you," Jesus says, "the Comforter will not come to you." This is one of the central mysteries of our human experience. We can only accept it in faith and celebrate it in love.

Being in the World

TIME: MAY 19, 1985

SEASON: SEVENTH SUNDAY OF EASTER

SCRIPTURE READINGS: ACTS 1:15–17, 20A, 20C–26;
    1 JOHN 4:11–16; JOHN 17:11B–19

Life in the world, for the world, but not of the world re-quires a consciousness that keeps us from being taken in by a value system influenced by ratings, instant pleasure, self-love, and violence. The truth of the world is that the Creator calls it forth in love as a sign of a deeper meaning, with a sacredness in its people and in its gardens. We are truly in each other's care, needing to grow in understanding, learning how to see and love the truth.

We have just heard some strange, complex, disturbing words in the Gospel, where Jesus refers to the disciples as "not of the world, no more than I am of the world." These are words about us. Jesus is praying for us to the Father. We are the ones who are in the world and so need God's protection from the evil one. We are the ones who live in the world but do not belong to it, any more than Jesus did, and yet we are the ones who are sent to the world, as Jesus was.

What does it mean not to belong to the world in which we live? Do you feel any sense of alienation, of being a strang-er in the world? We *should* feel uneasy and not completely at home here. Do you feel any sense of having been sent on mis-sion to this world to which you do not belong?

In the Gospel of John, "world" means all that stands against the Holy One: evil demonic powers, everything that refuses to accept the values of Jesus, the one whom God sent for the salvation of the world. There seems to be a great distance between our current understanding of the world, our openness to secular reality, our sensitivity to modern, non-Christian society on the one hand, and the attitude of the Johannine community on the other.

But the words we have heard today proclaim a message still valid for this era, for any era, for Christians who might be tempted to become naively optimistic about the world in which they live, ready to blindly accept and affirm its values without challenging them. It would be simple and neat if we could say that communism is the evil power in the world and that our mission from Christ is to conquer it. But it is not so simple and neat. We need to look at our own world, the world of which we are a part, to discover its values and how they affect us.

A study by the University of Michigan on sexual values was recently aired on prime time television. Sex was presented as being the most fun when it is done with someone to whom you are not married and is accompanied by violence. Within the last ten days both a parent and a family counselor called my attention to MTV. They were very critical of the association they saw there between sexuality and violence. I have not watched MTV. I can only suggest to young people who do watch it that you ask yourselves: Are these my values? Are these the values of Jesus? Is this the way the Lord wants me to understand human relationships?

In 1979 Christopher Lasch published a book titled *The Culture of Narcissism: American Life in An Age of Diminishing Expectations*. A few weeks ago, the retreat master for our priests' retreat made reference to this book, reminding us of the Greek myth of the young man who so falls in love with his own image reflected in the water that he drowns trying to embrace it. The Greeks named a flower after Narcissus and made it the symbol of death: Love of self is the flower of death.

Abbot Bonaventure argued with great force that we have a culture of death because no other age, no other society, has been taught the love of self as we have. I am reminded of the story of a young couple that was recently in the news. Both had promising careers and had decided they would not have any children so as to be free to pursue their careers to the top without delay—and also because, for the man, his wine cellar was most important, and the woman did not want to spoil her slender figure with a pregnancy.

This is the world whose values are in conflict with the values of Christ. We live in this world. Do we belong to it? It seems to me that we have three choices. We can choose to go along with the world and embrace its values, which means either convincing ourselves that there is no conflict between the world's values and our Christian commitment, or living with a split personality as followers of Christ on Sunday and followers of the world the other six days of the week. We can run away from the world, closing our eyes and ears, and try to live only in God and with God, like hermits or cloistered religious.

Our third choice is to be in the world and for the world as Jesus was, seeking to transform the world into the kingdom of God, however long that might take, however painful it might be. That means that we need to continually transform ourselves through ongoing conversion so that we may influence those around us to see and follow Christ's way.

I believe this is our vocation, the vocation of all who are called to live in the hustle and bustle of the world, jostled, harassed, sacrificed. If God were truly present only in the desert and in silence, then he would not be accessible to the majority of people today. And this would make the Incarnation a lie and a failure, because its purpose was to join Christ to humanity, to all of human life. As we heard today, the Father has sent the Son as Savior of the world. Ours task is to join Christ and human life, consciously and explicitly—his gospel, his values, his unconditional love joined to, active in, transforming first our life and then all of human life.

The second reading makes a powerful statement: "If we love one another God dwells in us, and his love is brought to perfection in us." God's love is made perfect in our love, in the love we have for one another. God is love, and if we abide in love we abide in God and God in us, and the prayer of Jesus for us will be fulfilled.

Filled with the Spirit

TIME: MAY 22, 1994

SEASON: THE FEAST OF PENTECOST

SCRIPTURE READINGS: ACTS 2:1–11;
    1 CORINTHIANS 12:3–7, 12–13; JOHN 20:19–23

Today we heard the work of the Spirit of God presented in three different scenes, from three different perspectives. In the first scene, from the Book of Acts, there is a powerful wind, a noise that fills the whole house, dancing tongues of fire, a phenomenon of foreign tongues and understanding, streets filled with people and thousands asking to be baptized. In this scene the manifestation of the Spirit is noisy, public, tangible, visible, accompanied by spectacular signs.

In the second scene, from the Gospel of John, Jesus enters quietly, almost surreptitiously. He speaks of peace, breathes softly, and sends the disciples to continue his work of forgiveness. A quiet scene, small and private, without any outward, visible signs of the passing on of Jesus' mission to the disciples. And Paul, writing to the fractious community of Christians in Corinth, who were fighting with each other over the relative importance of various gifts and ministries, reminds us of the work of the Spirit within each of us. We cannot even affirm the lordship of Jesus except in the Holy Spirit, and it makes no difference what gifts we have received, what ministries we exercise, because they are all from the same Spirit, and all for the common good.

There is a silent presence of the Spirit within our own spirit and heart, a gift we all have received. Our spirit longs for the touch of the Spirit of God. There is a hunger in us for beauty and love, for understanding and communion. Below all the surface glitter and postures of confidence, there is an emptiness, an ache in our hearts, a question: Does anyone really love me just for myself, not just for what I say and do? Does my life really matter to anyone? Is there someone who cares for me and who I am?

C.S. Lewis, in his autobiography, describes the awakening of his imagination as a child as the emerging "of an

unsatisfied desire which is itself more desirable than any other satisfaction." He calls this unsatisfied desire "joy."[26]

He is talking about an inner experience of a divine yearning, a reaching out for something beyond our ordinary life and our material world. In a culture seeking instant gratification and filled with constant distractions, I believe people feel this hunger even more deeply, although few may be able to name it.

Our spirit needs the touch of the Spirit of God to survive. Can you say "Jesus is Lord" and know the power of his presence and the impact of his sovereignty in your life and the longing for a deeper communion in his love? Can you call out "Abba, Father," and feel the overwhelming tenderness of God's love for you, his never-failing care for you? This is the work, these are the signs of the Spirit within you: You need only become more aware of her presence, more responsive to her urging to reach beyond all the passing things of this world, to reach for the ultimate beauty, love, understanding waiting for us in the mystery of God.

But all three readings today make very clear that the Spirit is never given just for our private purposes or personal satisfaction. The Spirit of Pentecost drives the disciples out into the streets to proclaim the story of Jesus. The gift of the Spirit by the Risen Christ in the Gospel of John is a charge to continue what Jesus had begun in the world, to continue his work of reconciliation.

Paul insists that that Spirit is never given just as a private source of information and inspiration, comfort and pride. The gifts of the Spirit are given to each person for the common good, to build the community, not to divide it and destroy it. He uses the powerful language of the human body to get his point across. Just like the body, which has many parts that all work together for the good of the body as a whole, the Christian community includes many diverse individuals who have been baptized into one body. Whether Jew or Greek, slave or free, all were members of the body of Christ. Today we would have to add: whether white or black, rich or poor, male or female, citizens of the Third World or of the developed world.

To argue about who has the better and greater gift of the Spirit works for disintegration. It is a betrayal of Christ's work of reconciliation and salvation. The work of Jesus was to integrate us once again, with each other and with God, to ground all of us again, all of creation, into the life-giving Spirit of God, that creative force from which we all originate, both individually and collectively.

> The consequences of this integration must be joy, relationship, growth, creative experiences, manifestations... of the creative spirit in each of us. [The scene in John's Gospel] stresses peace, mutual forgiveness, as a consequence of the Spirit's release, as evidence of the Spirit's arrival and presence in the world: personal and collective peace, mercy, love, the vital signs and energy of a redeemed humanity.[27]

In 1924, when people thought of the First World War as "the war to end all wars," William Butler Yeats wrote a poem titled "The Second Coming." Recently, in the euphoria following the breaking down of the Berlin Wall and the collapse of the communist governments in the Soviet Union and in Eastern Europe, we spoke with great confidence of a "new world order," of the triumph of capitalist democracy, and of a bright future for all the oppressed peoples of the world. But, as we have seen, ancient hatreds and modern greed have given us a far different reality. I was startled to realize how Yeats' words, written seventy years ago, ring true once again in our day:

> Things fall apart; the centre cannot hold;
> Mere anarchy is loosed upon the world;
> The blood-dimmed tide is loosed, and everywhere
> The ceremony of innocence is drowned;
> The best lack all conviction, while the worst
> Are full of passionate intensity.

We need to renew and deepen our conviction and be filled with the passionate intensity of the Spirit of God. The world desperately needs Spirit-filled people to shout the good news that there is something in us that transcends all barriers and divisions of class and race and language and gender and cultural differences: It is our unity as children of the same God.

Our challenge, as the Church of Jesus Christ, is to proclaim in our words and live in our life the truth that the love of God in all of us can speak louder than the gun and be more powerful than all our human divisions. We begin right here, by letting the Spirit of God fill our heart and spirit. For God has indeed sent forth his Spirit to renew the face of the earth, but the Spirit can only work his transforming grace through us.

What Kind of God Do We Seek?

TIME: JUNE 2, 1985
SEASON: TRINITY SUNDAY
SCRIPTURE READINGS: DEUTERONOMY 4:32–34, 39–40;
ROMANS 8:14–17; MATTHEW 28:16–20

Karl Rahner, one of the most influential theologians of the twentieth century, argues that human beings, by the very fact of their existence in this particular world and history, are always and inevitably more than mere natural beings, that all human beings stand under the universal saving will of God, that we are permanently the ones to whom God offers his loving care and the gift of his own personal love.

To put it in a different way: We live in a redeemed world, filled with the saving presence of God in Jesus Christ. From the very beginning of our existence, prior to any choice or decision on our part, the God who transcends all our categories of being and of thought, the God who is greater than all that we can experience or imagine, takes the initiative and offers us his grace, his love, the possibility of entering into an inner relationship with him, of participating in his divine life, of entering his very nature.

All of us, then, and perhaps everything that exists, are born with the tendency toward God, are given this longing and this possibility to go beyond ourselves, to reach out beyond the limits of our earthly powers to find a new dimension, to find God.

I believe that everyone, and everything, seeks God, is moved from within and yearns from the very heart of being to find the living God. Where does our search lead us? What is the object of our quest? What kind of God have we found?

Some of the gods we meet are false gods:

✝ the god who gives victory to the strong; the real God operates in weakness and meekness

✝ the god who makes prosperity a sign of his blessing; the real God takes the side of the poor

✝ the god who is the answer to fill the gaps of our ignorance; the real God is constant question and challenge

✝ the god of reason and philosophical systems; the real God finds the heart of marrow of humans

✝ the god of natural law and order; the real God is full of surprises and novelty

✝ the god who stands in the way of our freedom and who must be pushed aside; the real God calls us to freedom and responsibility

✝ the god of modern science and technology; the real God is discovered in loving human relationships

Look at the story of your own searching. Perhaps you will find some other false images of God, some other idols.

When we do meet the true God, what will we find?

✝ We will find a tender Father, who wants to be called Abba, Dad.

✝ We will find a compassionate brother who came to serve us.

✝ We will find a freedom-giving, liberating Spirit who gives us the very life that the Son shares with the Father.

The best faith experience does not try to claim too much for human knowledge of the transcendent God. It remains deeply respectful of the inscrutable mystery of God. It only tries to give the best expression that words and symbols and worship can give to the way God has touched us and made himself known to us.

To know God as Father and Creator means both to open our eyes to see and to appreciate the works of God's power, wisdom and affection, to treat with reverence all of creation and history, but also to know that we are creatures, to know God as the one in whom we live and move and have our being.

St. Augustine, in the *Confessions*, asks:

And what is God? I asked the earth, and it answered, 'I am not He,' and all therein made the same confession. I asked the sea, and the deeps, and the creeping things that lived, and they answered, 'We are not your God, seek higher than we.' I asked the winds, and the air which is everywhere, with all its inhabitants, answered, 'The philosopher was deceived; I am not God.' I asked the heavens, the sun, moon, and stars. 'Neither,' they said, 'are we the God whom you seek.' And I replied to all these things which stand above the door of my flesh: 'You have told me concerning my God that you are not he: tell me something about him.' And with a loud voice they exclaimed, 'He made us!' And the Father has made each of us.

To know the Son is to know the mystery of God-with-us in the person of Jesus. Through intimacy with Jesus, identifying closely with his life, his attitudes, his actions, participating in his death and resurrection through listening to his word and celebrating his sacraments, we come to know God as intimate, as a person related to us, as he who is with us always, until the end of time. He is with us as servant, calling us to mutual service. He is with us as the compassion of the Father, calling us to compassion for each other.

To know the Spirit is to know the divine life present in us, to be conscious of the divine offer of grace and love and able to accept it and respond to it. To know the Spirit is to know the personal intimacy of Father and Son as a gift they have shared with us. To know God as Spirit is to be lifted beyond the experiences of fear and slavish obedience to the law, to be lifted into the spontaneity and creativity that is testimony to our adoption as children of God, that energizes our human freedom—a liberating freedom, not self-destroying, self-defeating, self-justifying, but making us free to live for God and for others.

The Meaning of the Eucharist

TIME: JUNE 13, 1982
SEASON: BODY AND BLOOD OF CHRIST
SCRIPTURE READINGS: EXODUS 24:3–8; HEBREWS 9:11–15;
   MARK 14:12–16, 22–26

Our Scripture readings today are filled with references to the use of blood and its symbolism in the sealing and in the ritual re-enactment of both the ancient and the new covenant, through which our relationship with God is experienced and expressed.

In the twenty-fourth chapter of Exodus, two ceremonies for the ratification of the Sinai covenant are interwoven. The first ceremony, the eating of a meal, forms a frame for the passage we heard this morning, which describes the sealing of the covenant through the sprinkling of the blood.

In Hebrew thought and Scripture blood signifies life. In this story, the altar is the symbol of God, the twelve pillars represent the whole people of Israel. The blood of sacrificed animals is used as an expression of life, and that blood is sprinkled on the altar, on the pillars, and on the people, signifying that all now share the same life. Yahweh has committed himself to his people by the bond of his own free choice. The people commit themselves to live according to the Law they have received from the Lord. "All that the Lord has said, we will heed and do." The covenant is sealed in blood. This relationship between God and his people is a sharing of life.

The second reading, from the Letter to the Hebrews, echoes the covenant ratification ceremony from the book of Exodus. The letter may have been written for some Jewish Christians who missed and were longing for the rituals and sacrifices of the Jerusalem temple, which had probably been destroyed already by the time the letter was written, and who perhaps wanted to return to the ancient practices. The main concern of this writing is to show the superiority of the new covenant in Jesus Christ to the ancient covenant of Sinai. The sacrificial cult of the temple has been replaced by the sacrifice of Christ.

The Jewish High Priest had the right to enter the Holy of Holies in the temple because he bore the blood of the sacrificial animals. Jesus enters the heavenly sanctuary, the fullness of life and glory with the Father, not with the blood of animals but with his own blood. The sacrifice of Jesus on the cross, now made of eternal value by his resurrection and return to the Father's glory, has the power not only to give ritual cleansing, a proper status for participating in worship, but also to cleanse, purify, put at peace our conscience, to free our inner being, our very self from sin and all that is dead, that we may be alive in God. This is the new covenant.

And the Gospel reading from Mark tells us how the saving sacrifice of Jesus is perpetuated and made present, active, and effective for all his followers. Jesus, again in the context of a meal, as in the reading from Exodus, uses common elements from the table as the signs of his sacrifice, of his gift, which is our salvation. The bread, his body, the wine, his blood, say that he has given his whole self for our sake, and through his gift we have a new covenant, we enter a new relationship with him and with the Father. This is a sharing of life, his life, through his blood.

In the past fifteen years or so the sacrificial aspect of the Mass, of the Eucharistic liturgy, has been neglected. Our theology, our celebrating, our personal faith experience have been dominated by the aspect of the meal in the Eucharist. This shift in outlook was necessary, because for many years the meal dimension had been neglected and the notion of sacrifice had been the almost exclusive focus of Eucharistic devotion. We need to find a balance. The Eucharist is both meal and sacrifice. Our faith and our worship must embrace both.

Perhaps the notion of sacrifice needs reinterpretation. In the past we have thought of sacrifice too much as punishment, expiation, paying a price for sin. The cross was seen as the tragic ordeal that Jesus accepted in our place, to pay for all our sins. Today I believe that we find it more fruitful, more relevant to our experience, to think of sacrifice as giving up something so that others might have it, letting go of something that is ours so that others might be richer, accepting suffering when it becomes part of our service to others.

Jesus was willing to give up his life so that we might share in it. He did this not only by dying on the cross, but also with his whole life. The death on the cross was the inevitable result of the prior choice that Jesus had made: to put his life in the service of human beings and all creation, men and women of his time and all times, the choice not to be a triumphant king but to be a servant who makes possible a new way of being, who brings new hope for a new world, by giving himself totally into service—even if this leads to death on a cross.

The reality of this total gift, even his saving death, the reality of his sacrificial life as servant, is made present for us in the Mass, in the Eucharistic liturgy. He is here for us now, as he was for the disciples in the upper room, for the women at the foot of the cross.

What does this mean for us? To participate in a symbol is to commit ourselves to its meaning, to make it our own, to accept it for ourselves. Our participation in the Eucharist goes beyond the gesture of eating and drinking. It must draw us into the reality of the Lord's life and death. It is not only Christ saying, "This is my Body given for you . . . . This is my blood poured out for you." It must also be each of us saying, "This is my life given up, broken up for others." The bread that is broken must speak of our willingness to be broken ourselves for the sake of others, as Jesus was broken for the life of the world.

If we understand this, every reception of the Eucharist will be a humbling experience as we become more aware of the many ways in which we fail to live up to this ideal. We are not yet totally willing to let go of our life, to surrender ourselves to the many small deaths that confront us every day, if we put ourselves in the service of others.

But the Eucharist also tells us that after every death there is a possibility of life. Life is not limited. The life, death, and resurrection of Jesus tell us that giving up our life is not destroying it. The more we share, the more there is. Jesus willingly gives up his own life to create a new life for his friends, a life of new hopes and new dreams. Eating the body and drinking the blood of Jesus in the Eucharist, sharing in his sacrificial death, is the expression of our willingness, of our commitment, to give up our own life so that others may have life.

Planting the Seeds of the Kingdom

TIME: JUNE 16, 1991

SEASON: ELEVENTH SUNDAY IN ORDINARY TIME

SCRIPTURE READINGS: EZEKIEL 17:22–24; 2 CORINTHIANS 5:6–10;
MARK 4:26–34

We heard some poetic language and beautiful images in today's biblical readings, describing God's work and action in the world. The words of Ezekiel were addressed to the people of Judah living in exile in Babylon. They are a promise that God will bring them home again and re-establish the nation, the city, and the temple. The image used by the prophet to express this promise is that of a majestic cedar planted on the mountain heights. Think of the giant sequoias that grow so tall and big and strong on our mountains. Imagine how you would feel if someone, speaking as God's messenger, were to say to you: "That is how God will build you up, that is what God will make of your community!"

The Gospel has two images. The first one is the seed planted that mysteriously sprouts and grows and matures until harvest time. The message is that the reign of God is his work and not ours, that it grows mysteriously because of God's power and care, even when and where we would never suspect it.

In reading this, I was reminded of some of the trees and bushes that were hit by the freeze last December. They seemed to be completely dead, and we were beginning to talk about pulling them out and replacing them. But when we looked closely we saw that some tiny, almost invisible buds were beginning to sprout. After a while there were leaves and the bushes were green again. We did not do anything; it just happened. The power of life is so strong that it cannot be destroyed. It appears at times in the most unexpected places.

The second image is that of the tiny seed that grows up to be a large bush, large enough to give shade and support and shelter to birds and their nests. At a time when Jesus' ministry was being challenged and misunderstood and seemingly going nowhere, he wanted to give hope and courage to his disciples by telling them to be patient, to trust that the power of God can take even the smallest and shakiest beginnings and bring them to a successful outcome. That is the way God works; that is the way of the kingdom.

Is the seed of God's kingdom growing in our world? Do you see any signs of that mighty bush described by Jesus as an image of the reign of God that is supposed to provide shade and shelter and protection? I guess another way to ask the question would be: Do you think the world is better or worse than it was fifty, a hundred, two hundred years ago?

You hear many people say that things are worse, that our country is in decline, that we seem to be mired in more and more insoluble problems everywhere in the world. I think things are better, though not yet for all. Think about the slave trade, the horrors of child labor, the total disregard for human rights, the privileged few taking advantage of the miserable many. These problems are not all corrected completely and everywhere, but the world has improved and these evils bring forth outcries when they are discovered. There have been many famines in Africa, but never before such good will to help. There is still much injustice and exploitation, but never has there been a greater concern for the poor. Things are not worse, but our expectations are greater, for the very good reason that the seed has been growing and continues to grow among us.[28]

Here are some contemporary stories that I hope will reinforce the message we heard in the Gospel parables and renew us in hope and courage. There is much evidence of a decline and even death of faith in Europe. Only 7 percent of the French and 15 percent of the Italians practice their faith. The great cathedrals are filled only with tourists. Although many would still call themselves Catholic, many have abandoned their Catholic heritage. But two hours from Paris there is a community called L'Arche, which means ark and covenant in French.

> Founded by Jean Vanier, a Canadian layman, it is a community for mentally and physically disabled men and women who have been rejected by their family and societies. Few are turned away, and those accepted can stay as long as they want. L'Arche is now an international movement with houses in many parts of the world. At L'Arche residents are

joined by healthy, intelligent and dynamic young people who could succeed at anything but have come to give weeks, months and even years of service to the less fortunate. The disabled and healthy learn about each other by loving each other. L'Arche volunteers receive a priceless reward: they come to see God in the people they serve. . . . L'Arche is a welcoming vessel and a place where intense friendships are forged between people and God.[29]

Or we could talk about Taizé, the monastery founded by Protestants after World War II in France, which is now an ecumenical monastery. Although it was not planned this way, it has become a center of pilgrimage for youth. Young people, as many as four thousand a week, come from all over Europe to join the monks in prayer, to experience there a peace and unity they have never felt before. They come seeking the words of life, looking for real faith and something deeper in life than fame and money.

Here is another story, from Rome. It is about a community called San Egidio. It is a lay association that emphasizes prayer, service, and community. It began in the sixties, with students gathering for prayer and reflection. It has become a community of several thousand, who work at a variety of jobs, but also dedicate themselves to running a soup kitchen and a health clinic, teaching Italian to immigrants, helping battered women. At the end of the day they gather to pray in a church that is their meeting place. Pope John Paul II occasionally comes to pray with them. In recent years they have sent missioners to other European countries, Africa, and Latin America.

In Saginaw, Michigan, Bishop Untener has asked all parishes, all organizations and groups in the diocese, to ask this question about every decision they make: How will this affect the poor? The whole diocese is experiencing a profound renewal and conversion.

And what about our own Poverello House? This growing program that feeds and cares for Fresno's street people began as a tiny seed, with sandwiches and chili beans being passed out to the hungry from the trunk of a car.

All these are the tiny seeds of God's just and peaceful kingdom, which the Lord nurtures and makes grow until the time of the harvest.

Keeping Our Stuff Together

TIME: JUNE 30, 1991

SEASON: THIRTEENTH SUNDAY IN ORDINARY TIME

SCRIPTURE READINGS: WISDOM 1:13–15, 2:23–24;
2 CORINTHIANS 8:7, 9, 13–15; MARK 5:21–43

A little boy asked his mother what happens to people when they die. The mother, using the best traditional theology, told him that the body is buried in the ground but the soul goes to heaven to be with God. And the boy replied, "That's OK, but I'd rather keep my stuff together!"

There seems to be an original, profound, irresistible need and drive in everything to "keep our stuff together," to achieve and maintain a wholeness and unity of being against every attempt to break it down, to dissolve it. There is no being that wants simply to die, that does not resist death. At least this is the way Western thought has understood and interpreted reality. Today's reading from the book of Wisdom seems to confirm this view. Even God does not want living things destroyed; he did not make death, and he created man and woman to be imperishable, in the image of his own eternal reality.

And yet there is death. Why? The book of Wisdom blames the envy of the devil and the sin of Adam and Eve for death entering the world. But that story is a mythical, symbolic way of recognizing human freedom, human sinfulness, and the ways in which we humans are responsible for a great deal of evil, cruelty, pain, and death in the world. Isn't the possibility of moral evil intrinsic to the very nature of freedom? If we want a world in which there is true freedom, we have to accept the possibility of its misuse.

What about natural evils? Could a material world be created in such a way that there would be no volcanoes erupting, no earthquakes or floods, no cyclones or tornadoes, no droughts? Can you imagine material things like crops or human-made machines, or even our bodies, in which there would be no breakdown, no wearing out, no aging, no accidents, no natural disasters, no death, no suffering? I cannot imagine this.

I cannot imagine a world in which matter and freedom are essential elements that would be free from evil and death. Can you imagine a world with freedom and matter that would be much different structurally from the world in which we live? I cannot. Could God have created a different world, a world in which there were no evil, no death? I don't know. That is the ultimate, final question in our struggle to understand the reality of evil, and I have not found an answer. From a rational, logical perspective I would want to say, however, that a world free from evil and death could not include freedom and matter as we know it. But that's enough philosophy for a hot summer day! This is the world we have, this is all we have to work with—and so does God.

Given the world as we know it, how do we deal with evil and death? First of all we must recognize the reality of evil and pain and suffering and death, and not deny it or romanticize it. One of the speakers at a colloquium I attended in May on "The American Way of Dying" was very eloquent in arguing that the purpose of all that we do and are is to give glory to God. Death, like life, must give glory to God, he said. But another participant immediately remarked that she found it very difficult to see how a baby dying with AIDS would give glory to God. And she insisted that there is a tragic and dark element to death. Death is failure and defeat. We have a right to feel strongly that this is not the way it should be. We have to deal with our own pain and grief and anger.

Clearly, we need to ask how God deals with death and evil, pain and disorder and tragedy. If I read the book of Wisdom correctly, God struggles with death along with us. He does not rejoice in the destruction and death of things. God has not changed his plan to make man and woman in his own image, to make them imperishable. As he did for his beloved Son, Jesus Christ, so he does with each of us and each of his creatures. He suffers death with us because death is the inevitable destiny of all things in this world of ours, but then transforms death into new and glorious life. I love the imagery and the language of Paul. He compares death and burial to burying a seed in the ground. What is born, what arises is intimately connected, of the same nature as the seed that was buried, but also radically different. He writes:

> So it is with the resurrection of the dead. What is sown is perishable, what is raised is imperishable. It is sown in dishonor, it is raised in glory. It is sown in weakness, it is raised in power. It is sown a physical body, it is raised a spiritual body. (1 Cor. 15:42–44)

There is the new and different world that God is in the process of creating, where there is no death, no pain, no tears, no evil. But that seems in many ways distant and far away. How do we, how does God, deal with evil and death here and now, in this world? Look at the stories we read from the Gospel of Mark today, the stories of the healing of Jairus' daughter and the woman suffering from hemorrhages.

That is how God, personally present in our world in Jesus Christ, responds to suffering, pain, and death. By healing and calling back to life, by restoring relationships. He answers with love, empathy, and compassion, sharing the pain and the burden—not afraid to shatter prejudice and break conventions, not afraid to be touched by someone in pain, not afraid to enter the space where death is to challenge its hold. There is an aspect of the Gospel story that is not immediately evident.

In the inner story, we hear about a woman who had been afflicted with a hemorrhage for a dozen years. That meant that for all this time, according to Levitical law, she was ritually unclean. She was not able to enter a place of worship or touch anything having to do with worship, and anyone who touched her would also become unclean. The woman was forced into isolation by fear and rejection because of her bleeding. She was desperate, and in her desperation, she did the forbidden thing: she touched Jesus. She was healed, but he became ritually unclean. That is why she tried to hide and get away as quickly as possible. But Jesus seeks her out, and she comes forward in fear and trembling. You can almost hear her apologizing: "Forgive me for having touched you, for having made you unclean. Forgive me for bothering you, for wanting to be healed; forgive me for being a woman."

But Jesus is not concerned about his ritual defilement. There is not a word about the law, or its consequences. He only says: "My daughter, your faith has restored you to health. Go in peace." By the healing, by his acceptance and affirmation of her faith and her being, Jesus restores the woman to the possibility of life and relationships, to wholeness and total health.

That is how God deals with evil and pain and death, and that is how he calls us to deal with our world. None of us are strangers to pain and fear and death. We need to feel Jesus' touch even as the woman touched his garment, as the little girl felt the touch of his hand on hers. We need to hear Jesus calling us to rise up, affirming our faith, and saying to us: "Fear is useless; what is needed is trust." Trust in him and in the God who sent him, the God who did not make death but formed us to be imperishable.

The Power of Weakness

TIME: JULY 7, 1991

SEASON: FOURTEENTH SUNDAY IN ORDINARY TIME

SCRIPTURE READINGS: EZEKIEL 2:2–5; 2 CORINTHIANS 12:7–10;
    MARK 6:1–6

The second reading today, from Paul's second letter to the church in Corinth, contains one of the most paradoxical and challenging statements in the Bible: that power reaches perfection in weakness, that it is when we are powerless that we are strong.

I am sure that the idea that power is exercised in weakness, that powerlessness becomes strength, was as startling and as counter-cultural in the time of Paul as it is in our time. Then, as now, power was exercised through strength. The Romans controlled Palestine through military power, and the Sadducees and Pharisees tried to manipulate the Roman occupation forces through influence, in order to maintain their privileged status. Weakness was despised and the powerless were trampled.

Paul is writing to defend himself and his apostolic credentials against a group of people who were trying to control the church in Corinth by boasting of their superior credentials, of their eloquence in preaching, of their visionary revelations and their miraculous powers. Paul answers them by boasting of his weaknesses and the hardships, the failures, he has endured for the sake of the gospel, because it is in these that the power of the crucified and risen Christ is revealed and works out the community's salvation.

Sarcastically, Paul makes reference to his visionary experiences but, in the same breath, notes that the Lord let him continue to suffer with some physical defect or illness, no matter how much he prayed to be set free from this weakness and impediment to his apostolic work. Paul is content with "weakness, insults, hardships, persecutions and constraints . . . ." These are the true signs of the apostle who follows the crucified Jesus and allows God's power to work through human weakness.

Ezekiel was deported to Babylon by Nebuchadnezzar, together with the king, Jehoiachin, and thousands of the leading citizens of Jerusalem, during the first wave of exile, in 597. It was there that he received his prophetic call from the Lord, in 593, seven years before the fall of Jerusalem, and before the destruction of the temple, in 586. After a spectacular vision of the glory of God, a humbled Ezekiel is asked to face a rebellious Israel, and to announce that their persistent sin will cause the destruction of the city and its temple. This was the first message he had to deliver as he faced the hardness of heart and the rejection of the people.

After he receives news of the fall of Jerusalem in 586 B.C.E. (Ezek. 33), Ezekiel's oracles become constructive and life-giving. In hopeful visions of unforgettable poignancy, he speaks of Israel being revived with a new heart (chap. 36) and re-awakening like a valley of dry bones (chap. 37). His message concludes with visions of a new temple, land and community where the evils of the past have been removed (Ezek. 40–48). These hopeful visions strengthened the returning exiles as they rebuilt the nation and the temple in the last years of the sixth century B.C.E.[30]

This was his second message: God can rebuild his people out of defeat and humiliation, when everything seems lost and destroyed, when they seem to be at their lowest and weakest point and have no power left.

But the most striking revelation of how God's power works through weakness is Jesus Christ. The God of glory, the king of kings, is born a helpless human baby, just like the rest of us, needing to be fed, bathed, diapered. No one has ever met a self-sufficient human baby! Many of the world's hero-legends attempt to avoid this basic, uncomfortable fact by having the hero or heroine appear full grown, or born able to talk, work, fight. In the Gospel of John we see a reflection of this attitude. Jesus is first of all from God, and only incidentally from Nazareth. His "hometown" is the heavenly realm, his family is God, and so it does not matter much how his earthly family and hometown receive him.

In the other Gospels Jesus is born as a helpless, totally dependent human infant. When he grows up he associates with a marginal man who has come out of the desert to call people to change their lives, a counter-cultural man who is imprisoned and decapitated because of his challenge to authority.

In his preaching, Jesus uses the helpless, powerless, human child as a model of the attitudes that are necessary for being part of God's kingdom. After demonstrations of the power of God at work in him in the exorcism of the Gerasene demoniac, the raising of the daughter of Jairus, and the cure of the woman with the hemorrhage, Jesus comes to his town and his family and relatives, but he is rejected, because he is thought of as being ordinary, just like they are. Where does Jesus get his power, when they are so powerless?

But Jesus has a different kind of power, a saving power that is used only for others, not for himself, a transforming power that operates in tenderness and compassion, not in force and coercion, a power that is manifested and reaches its fulfillment in weakness, in the acceptance of suffering and death, not by imposing itself upon others. Jesus rejects the use of power as the culture understands it, in the story of his temptation in the desert and in the reality of his daily life. He accepts suffering and death, trusting in the power of God to save him. And God vindicates him not by destroying his enemies but by raising Jesus to new life and empowering him to share that new life with all human beings and with the world.

It is only by accepting God's weakness in Jesus Christ that we will be able to accept our own weakness, and the weakness of the people and institutions around us. And it is only by accepting our weakness that we will be able to let the power of God work in us and reach its perfection.

The Nature of Our Calling

TIME: JULY 14, 1991

SEASON: FIFTEENTH SUNDAY IN ORDINARY TIME

SCRIPTURE READINGS: AMOS 7:12–15; EPHESIANS 1:3–14;
  MARK 6:7–13

I see a powerful sweep of history and a continuity of thought in the three Scripture readings today. We begin with Amos, who tells the high priest at the king's temple: "Look, I didn't want to be here either. I am not a prophet, and I didn't want to be one. I did not go to any prophetic school. I am just a shepherd and an orchard worker, and the Lord grabbed me and sent me here and said to me, 'Go, prophesy to my people Israel.' So don't tell me not to prophesy here. I don't care if it is a royal temple, I have to do what the Lord sends me to do."

This is another story of a very ordinary guy whom the Lord chooses as his agent and messenger. The Lord does not seem to have any special preferences for highly educated or well placed or well-to-do or highly talented people. Perhaps you yourself have experienced God speaking to you, you have seen the Spirit at work—in a grandparent who did not have much formal training in faith or anything else, in a child whose unspoiled freshness and enthusiasm is not yet an obstacle to God's action, in a student—not always the brightest, in someone who is poor and struggling to survive. Yes, God has the habit of calling on plain, ordinary people just like you and me to proclaim his message, to do his work.

The second reading tells us exactly that: We have been chosen by God for a special gift and task. No, the passage does not mean that we were programmed from all eternity, without any regard for our freedom, without any choice left to us. And no, Paul is not talking about predestination in the way later Calvinistic theology understood it. It does not mean that we were chosen by God for salvation, while others are chosen or predestined for damnation.

Paul, with extraordinary beauty and power, tells us that we were chosen to know Jesus Christ and the mystery of God's salvation in him; that we were chosen to be holy and blameless in his sight and full of love; that we were chosen to continue Christ's mission, to bring all things into one under his authority, to empower everyone to receive and to praise God for the divine gift of reconciliation, peace, and salvation that he has bestowed on all of us in his beloved Son. We have received an extraordinary gift and grace from God, through no merit of our own, and this gift and grace carry a wonderful, and in some ways dreadful, responsibility for us who have accepted the call to be disciples of Jesus and workers in God's kingdom, as he was.

And the Gospel tells us what that responsibility is, and what the conditions are for our carrying out our task. Last Sunday's Gospel focused on the reception, or rejection, of Jesus within his own community, his hometown and family. In the Gospel of Mark, this may be symbolic of the Jerusalem and Palestinian community. In today's Gospel reading, the disciples are sent to outsiders. The community that gave us the Gospel of Mark was expanding its missionary range and moving into Gentile lands.

There are two significant differences in this story as found in Mark and in the other two Synoptic Gospels, Matthew and Luke. In contrast to the other writers, Mark allows the disciples to wear sandals, perhaps because they are going to travel greater distances, and to carry a staff, indicating that such traveling would entail great personal danger. But for everything else the disciples on their missionary journeys are to rely completely on the Lord and his power, not on the baggage and tools and resources that they can take with them. And so, in a way, we are back to Amos. The first disciples, like the ancient prophet, go out because they are sent. They face rejection, opposition and great danger; they must trust completely in the Lord who empowers them for their mission.

And this brings us to ourselves, because the summons and the sending did not stop with the twelve or with the community of Mark, but continues even to this very Sunday. We are the ones who have been summoned and who will be sent forth at the end of Mass. This raises a host of questions. Are we willing to accept, are we prepared for the task of advancing the presence of God's kingdom? Are we willing to travel light enough to keep up with the insistent presence of God that urges us on? What possessions encumber us on our journey of evangelization? What does it mean to tell the story of Jesus in our world, and what are the conditions that will make our telling of the story effective? How aware are we of the cultural and historical issues that condition the proclamation of the kingdom of God? Does the way we live give witness to, or contradict, the very story we are trying to communicate?

These are mostly personal questions, ones that each of us must answer for ourselves. There are other questions that perhaps call for more general answers. Jesus sent the disciples forth with authority over evil spirits, to cast out demons, to heal and cure, to call people to repentance. How do we translate this mission for those of us who live in North America, in California, during the 1990s? Can we name the demons of our time?

I am sure all of us would come up with different lists, but I would like to make some suggestions to stimulate your thinking. One demon is surely "addiction"—not just drug addiction, which is certainly a demon, but all the forms of addictive behavior that enslave us: power, money, and possessions; the desire and drive to possess and consume more and more; the myth of progress understood as material growth; sex as a plaything, and the search for instant pleasure and gratification; and many more.

I would name another demon our "culture of violence." The Senate Judiciary Committee recently labeled us "the most violent country on earth." Its report states: "In 1990 the United States led the world with its murder, rape and robbery rates. When viewed from the national perspective, these crime rates are sobering. When viewed from the international perspective, they are truly embarrassing."[31] I was shocked when I read that we have more people in prison in California than in all of England and Italy put together, and we continue to build more prisons.

A third demon of our time I would call our "cultural wasteland," using the regular offerings of TV entertainment as a symbol of the emptiness of mind and waste of time on which so many of our citizens, young and old alike, spend precious hours.

In a recent speech, Archbishop Weakland raised the question of the crisis of culture in the Catholic Church, pointing to our so-called Catholic TV programs, such as the Eternal Word Television Network of Mother Angelica, as an example of the anti-intellectualism and lack of Catholic culture in this country. And that's all there is![32]

And how well are we moving to heal the sick? The ordinary way for healing today is through medical care. What are we doing, as disciples of Jesus, to challenge our society to move toward comprehensive medical programs so that everyone, not just those who are well off or insured, will have access to good basic health care?

As disciples of Jesus we are sent forth to challenge our world to repentance, to change our way of life so that the kingdom of God may be established in our midst. We are sent forth to exorcise and expel, from ourselves and from our society, the demons that possess us and threaten to destroy us. We are sent forth to bring the healing love and power of Christ for the spirit and the body, the minds and the hearts of our brothers and sisters. We gather to be nourished by the Word of God and the Bread of Life, so that at the end of our celebration we may go forth from here to carry out the mission entrusted to us by the Lord.

Getting Away from It All

TIME: JULY 20, 1997 (CAMP LA SALLE, HUNTINGTON LAKE)
SEASON: SIXTEENTH SUNDAY IN ORDINARY TIME
SCRIPTURE READINGS: JEREMIAH 23:1–6; EPHESIANS 2:13–18;
    MARK 6:30–34

"Come away and rest a while." The Gospel invitation seems most appropriate for this beautiful place in the mountains on this warm July Sunday. The need to leave the hectic pace of our regular life, to find a place of peace and quiet, to rest, to rebuild our strength, to reflect, is an essential need for our physical, emotional, and spiritual life. We have come here this morning, to this quiet place, to be with the Lord, to be nurtured and refreshed by God's Word and by the Bread of Life.

The disciples of Jesus have just returned from the mission on which they were sent by Jesus in last Sunday's Gospel reading. They are all excited because of the wonderful things that have happened to them, but they are also exhausted. They have had no time to rest, no time to eat. In the thirty-five years since the Second Vatican Council we have learned how critical a time to reflect on our ministry is for the vitality of that ministry. We need to ask regularly how we are doing, why we are doing it, whether it is the Lord's ministry, and how it is affecting the people whom we are trying to serve, as well as ourselves.

Quiet time is difficult to come by, as we heard in the Gospel today. The people get to the place ahead of them and are waiting for Jesus and the disciples. Jesus responds by having compassion on the people "because they were like sheep without a shepherd, and he began to teach them at great length." The image of the shepherd dominates the scripture readings today, especially the first reading and the Gospel.

In ancient Israel, as in all the cultures of the Near East, the figure of the king and the shepherd are closely associated. We heard Jeremiah criticize and condemn King Zedekiah and the recent kings of Judah for their neglect of their flock, the people of Judah, and their malfeasance in government, which resulted in the destruction of Jerusalem and the exile in

Babylonia. Jeremiah's message is that Yahweh will take back his flock, he will shepherd his people, he will rescue them and he will send a new righteous ruler, who will lead his people according to the mind and heart of Yahweh. This promise was soon interpreted as a reference to an ideal king who would restore the glory of Israel, leading later to the expectation of the Messiah king. For us the promise in Jeremiah has become a reality in Jesus: He is our Good Shepherd.

The royal theology of Judah found no contradiction between the notion that both Yahweh and the king were Israel's shepherds, for the king was the sacramental embodiment of Yahweh's kingship and shepherdhood. Christian faith sees the same dual notion fulfilled in Jesus Christ.[33]

We are called to continue the mission of Jesus, to be shepherds. Our initiation into the community of discipleship, our incorporation into the living Body of Christ by our baptism, the sharing of the Eucharist, and the gift of the Spirit challenge us to be shepherds in the midst of God's people, for the sake of the world, as Jesus was. We have always applied the image of the shepherd to the Pope, the bishops, and the priests. The parish priest is called pastor, which is the Latin word for shepherd. But the role is not limited to the ordained ministry; all of us are called to be shepherds.

Look for a moment to the biblical notion of the shepherd. What does Jesus do in today's Gospel? He begins to teach at length. How many of us are called to teach, in one way or another? Certainly, all of you who are parents, all of you who are professional teachers, and all of us who in so many ways are called to share our knowledge, our understanding of problems, our insights into people. All of us are called to share our knowledge of Jesus as the Lord and Savior of the world, wherever we are.

I mentioned that the figure of the shepherd was often associated with the king, with the exercise of authority, governance, leadership. Again, it seems to me that all of us have to exercise some authority over some people, whether it is in the home, or at work. Even children have leadership roles toward one another, especially the older ones toward the younger ones.

If we look at our responsorial Psalm, the Lord is my shepherd, we find enumerated a number of the functions Yahweh performs in his relationship with his people. I will just mention them, and I invite you to reflect on the ways in which you are called to do these things in your life, in your relationships with other people.

Yahweh nurtures, nourishes, guides his people, leads them to rest and refreshment. Yahweh comforts, encourages, empowers, takes away fear, even the fear of darkness and death. Yahweh anoints with oil, the ancient sign of commissioning and sending forth, just as we are called to pass on to new generations the traditions we have received and the powers of grace and life that have been entrusted to us.

If we look at the second reading, from the Letter to the Ephesians, we return to the constant theme of peace and reconciliation. The heart of the message of this marvelous document of Christian Scriptures is the discovery that God has broken down the barriers that separated Jews and Gentiles, those who were always near to God and those who were far away, but who now have been called to share the same mystery: In Christ we all have access to the same Father in the one Spirit. In Jesus we are enabled to reach a new depth in our relationship with God, and we are called to lead others to new insights into the mystery of God's love for all his children. Reginald Fuller expresses this new insight in these words: "Christ on the cross (i.e., by his death as the event of salvation) has fulfilled and abolished the law, not as a moral demand, but as the way of salvation: Christians now keep the law *because* they have been saved by grace, not *in order* to earn salvation."[34]

By his cross Jesus, our Good Shepherd, has saved us. By laying down his life for his flock, he has called us to share his *pastoral* ministry, his ministry as a shepherd. We are not substitutes for the presence of Christ, but the human vehicle through whose functions Christ renders himself present.[35]

Jesus has compassion on us this morning, as he had on the crowd that was pressing on him from every side. He teaches us through his holy word, he prepares a banquet for us in the

Eucharist, in which he offers us himself as the Bread of Life and the cup of salvation. And having taught us and nourished us, he will send us forth to minister to one another, as he did during his earthly life and continues to do now as the Risen Lord.

Liberal and Conservative: Can They Meet?

TIME: JULY 25, 1976

SEASON: SEVENTEENTH SUNDAY IN ORDINARY TIME

SCRIPTURE READINGS: 2 KINGS 4:42–44; EPHESIANS 4:1–6;
   JOHN 6:1–15

Twice today we hear of God's concern for the poor and the hungry: through the prophet Elisha and in the person of Jesus. Certainly this would seem to be a clear indication to us to share the same concern. Whatever miracle it is going to take to feed the billions of hungry people in the world today, we are to be part of it in one way or another. But it is not this participation and responsibility on which I would like to focus today. I would rather try to discuss the fact that how we accept this responsibility, how we try to respond to this need, can be profoundly divisive both for the Roman Catholic Church and for the whole Christian community.

To put the issue in broader terms: Social issues, social problems, the balance between political action and religious life, create deep divisions between liberal and conservative elements in all churches. The person of strong liberal tendencies will be involved in programs of social change and political action and public demonstrations, if necessary, in the name of Christianity, for the sake of the kingdom of God, for the establishment of justice and peace here and now. For the liberal, anyone in the Church who does not similarly become involved in social and political action is a "false Christian."

On the other hand, the person with strong conservative views will feel that religion should be mostly concerned with proper worship, with life in the sacraments, with personal morality, with obedience to both ecclesiastical and civil authorities, with prayer and with the giving of alms. And, of course, the conservative looks upon the activities of the liberal as subversive, dangerous to the peace of the country, and destructive of true religion.

To give a concrete example: Our choice of sending money, through the blue box, to the poor here and abroad is a conservative act. The liberal choice would be to become actively involved in efforts that will change the social conditions of poverty. This is nothing new in the church. The Letter to the Ephesians addresses itself to the same kind of condition in the church of the first century. The letter is an attempt to resolve a situation of great tension and conflict, and for that it is at times called "the great epistle of Christian unity."

We might even see a similarity between our situation and the two groups that contrast each other at Ephesus: the Jews and the Greeks. The Jews would be the conservatives. The Jews in Ephesus who have converted to Christianity want to remain by themselves, to hold on to their traditions, to keep themselves unspotted by the world. They look with great concern and disgust upon the Gentile converts who continue to live the life of the world, who remain part of their world and culture.

Paul insists, as we have seen now for several Sundays, that the mystery of God's plan and purpose was to unite all things in Christ, in the fullness of time. Last Sunday we heard Paul say that Christ has reconciled both Jews and Gentiles in his blood. He has broken down the wall of hostility and brought together into one both those who are far off, the Gentiles, and those who are near, the Jews.

In today's reading, the author of the Letter to the Ephesians pleads with both factions in the church at Ephesus to live a life worthy of this unity to which they have been called. Unity does not happen automatically. The Christians at Ephesus must work for it in humility, in meekness, in patience, in loving mutual forbearance.

Can the liberal and the conservative in the Church today learn to live in peace, harmony, and unity? Perhaps the experience of Jesus himself can teach us something in this respect. It should teach us at least this much: that neither side, neither conservative nor liberal, has a monopoly on a true understanding of the meaning of Jesus. Jesus himself experienced the same kind of tension we experience between living in and being part of this world and living with a perspective, a world view, that goes beyond this world.

If you remember the days of Jesus in the desert, you recall that he refused the temptation to use his power to become a political messiah, to turn stones into bread or to do things just to attract attention to himself. He refused to take over the kingdoms of the world, even for the purpose of making them into the kingdom of God. And yet, as often as he is confronted with sick people, with people in pain, with people held captive by some malevolent force, with people who are hungry for words and for bread, he uses his powers to cure the sickness, to relieve the pain, to feed the hunger. In today's Gospel, he refuses a political solution when the people come looking for him, to make him king.

The liberal wants to see service here and now as the sign of the kingdom. Jesus did just that. The conservative wants to emphasize the importance of prayer and worship, to say that the world here and now is not the only dimension, and Jesus did that as well.

The Christian life needs a balance of both involvement and detachment, of good works and prayer. Both are important. Can the liberals and the conservatives balance each other out, help one another to see both sides and dimensions of the Christian faith? Can they prevent one another from becoming completely one-sided?

Will the liberal learn from the conservative that government action does not solve all problems, that personal, individual action is also needed to relieve hunger and ease pain? Will the conservative learn from the liberal that anticommunism does not sum up and exhaust Christian activity and involvement, that technical assistance and unselfish sharing of material goods also must be part of the solution to world hunger?

I think this will happen only if we find some way to communicate with one another, only if we speak and listen to one another with respect, only if are open enough to appreciate the values stressed by the other, only if we try to reconcile these issues in the unity of Christ.

We need to work for this unity as Paul called the Ephesians to work for unity, in the same spirit that he described, in humility rather than arrogance. I can hold onto my convictions very firmly and set my life by them, but I cannot claim that I alone possess the absolute truth and the ultimate interpretation of the meaning of Christianity.

We need to meet one another with meekness rather than violence. We can discuss and disagree, but without personal attack and without immediately condemning the other as a "false Christian" simply because he disagrees with us or responds differently to the Christian vocation. We must do it in patience, with a willingness to wait for one another. We must deal with one another in loving, mutual forbearance, rather than intolerance.

Look at Paul again, in the second reading. I'd like to read it again, with some paraphrasing and commentary.

> We must make every effort to preserve the unity which has the Spirit as its origin and peace as its binding force. There is but one Body (Christ's risen body, the head of our organic union in Him), one spirit (the Spirit of God, not so much as a separate person, but as the intimate, immanent presence of God as He gives himself to us personally and to his community), one hope (the hope for a share in the resurrection of Jesus in the final coming of His Kingdom), one Lord (Jesus Christ), one faith (that Jesus is Lord), one baptism (through which all of us have been incorporated into the one body of Christ), one God who has shown himself as the Father to all who works through all (in spite of all our differences).

Even our multiplicity, our diversity, our pluralism are made one by our relation to the unique oneness of God.

I would like to call your attention to the small boy in today's story, as told somewhat differently in the Gospel of John. He contributes all he has, loaves and fishes, for the sake of all. Some commentators have suggested that the miracle in the multiplication of the loaves of bread was that Jesus succeeded in moving and motivating the people to share whatever provisions they had brought, to share with one another, so that there would be enough for everybody. I don't know how well that interpretation corresponds to the reality of the event, but I think it is a very compelling interpretation for our time. We need to share, not only our bread, but also our visions, our convictions, our faith, just as we are about to share the bread of unity which is the Eucharist. May God bless us.

Come Away for a While

TIME: AUGUST 4, 1991

SEASON: EIGHTEENTH SUNDAY IN ORDINARY TIME

SCRIPTURE READINGS: EXODUS 16:2–4, 12–15;
EPHESIANS 4:17, 20–24; JOHN 6:24–35

At the end of last Sunday's Gospel we saw Jesus slipping away from the crowd that wanted to make him king and going off by himself. As soon as the crowd realized that he had disappeared and where he had gone, they chased after him and, as you just heard, they found him on the other side of the lake, in Capernaum. What follows in the Gospel reading is a typical Johannine dialogue between Jesus and the crowd.

It is difficult to discern the original words of Jesus in these dialogues as reconstructed in the Gospel of John. The reason is that for the Johannine community, the community of the Gospel of John, the Risen Jesus is so immediately, intimately present to them that the dialogue is still going on between themselves and Jesus, and the content of what Jesus says is just as much a response to the present needs of the community as the words spoken by the earthly Jesus were a response to the situation in his day.

Our task is to continue that dialogue and bring it up to today. The Risen Lord is present in our midst just as much as he was for the Johannine community, and he wants to engage us in conversation and reflection, that we may understand him better, that we may be more open to the gift he brings us from the Father.

Look at what happens in the Gospel dialogue. The people begin with a rather banal question: "When did you get here?" Jesus does not bother to answer the question, but forces them to look at the real question: Why are they looking for him?

There is a hidden agenda; the people want more than bread. Jesus tells them: "You should not be looking for ordinary, perishable food for the body, but for what will give you eternal life and nourish it in you." "What do we have to do to get this eternal life?" the people ask. "Believe in me as the one whom

God has sent," answers Jesus. "How can we believe in you? How do we know that God has sent you?" Jesus insists that he is the real bread from heaven, the Bread of Life, that satisfies all hungers. He asks the people to come to him, to believe in him. "Sir, give us this bread always," the people beseech him.

Here we are now, and Jesus, the Risen Lord, is in our midst. Perhaps we did not give him much thought during the week. We were busy with work and family and home and making a living and having fun, and all the other important things in our life. But we have come here to be with the Lord today. Why are we here? Do we know what we are really looking for in Jesus, in worship, in prayer?

Jesus tells us: Look at your heart, look at your deepest longing and need. It is not for material things and bodily satisfaction and worldly success. Your strongest need is for God, for his presence, for his truth, his love within you, for an intimacy with God more immediate, deeper than any human intimacy, for a sharing of life with God that makes you one with him. Come to me, Jesus tells us, believe in me, trust in me with your whole self, with your heart and spirit, and I will lead you to God who gives you fullness of life.

This is what God was asking of the people of Israel in the desert, as we heard in the reading from Exodus this morning. The food and water they received from God were not just needed nourishment for the body, but also signs of God's presence with them, signs that they truly were God's people and that he was their God, signs of the covenant that united them in a binding, loving, demanding life relationship with God.

They were signs that the people should trust God completely, and the instructions on how they were to gather the manna makes this clear: They were to gather only enough for one day, except on Friday, when they gathered for two days because of the Sabbath. If they gathered more it would rot. You can't hoard the gifts of God; you have to trust that his gifts, his loving care, will still be there for you tomorrow.

The Letter to the Ephesians makes the same kind of appeal to the people who had recently accepted Christ. They cannot be just the same as they were before, just the same as everyone around them. They have to lay aside the old self and acquire a fresh, spiritual way of thinking. The dialogue, the symbolism, the appeal are as fresh, as relevant, and as urgent for us today as they were when first spoken. What does it mean for us to believe in Jesus, to bring our whole self to him, to develop a spiritual way of thinking?

First of all, it means that we have to be convinced that we cannot do it all by ourselves. We cannot have total control of our life, we cannot find fullness of life and deep peace and true happiness in ourselves, in other humans, in material things alone. We cannot "save" ourselves, if salvation means whole-ness of life, fulfillment of our search for meaning and peace, for beauty and truth, for trust and love, for the greatest possi-ble satisfaction of all our potential and possibilities. Salvation is from God alone, from his power and love, and he has made it available for us in his beloved Son, Jesus Christ. To him we must entrust our whole life and being.

Second, we need to ask: How much time and energy do we spend nurturing the life of our spirit, the life of faith and love and union with God in Jesus Christ? Today many of us understand the spiritual life in a very encompassing sense. As human beings we are one whole, a unity of spirit and matter, and we cannot isolate one from the other. The way I feel phys-ically affects the way I am able to be present to God as well as to others. My psychological, emotional state touches every-thing that I do, including my prayer life.

So I do not want to isolate the aspects of prayer, medita-tion, reading the Bible and other spiritual books, as if they were the only dimensions in our life that are spiritual, but I do want to say that these are essential aspects of a full human life, that physical and emotional well-being, professional compe-tence, attention to our human responsibilities, being informed about the important issues of the day, are not enough.

The only way to come to Jesus, to believe in him, is to know him more and more, to open our minds and our hearts to his word, to the example of his life, to give him adequate time and space in our life. I don't know how we can do that without reading, studying, praying the Bible, especially the

Gospels. I don't know how we can enter into the intimacy of God's life in us without some silence in our life, without some quiet time given to God. One of the most powerful lines in the Bible is the one from Psalm 46:10: "Be still and know that I am God." It is possible to find God in the midst of frantic activity, but often so difficult, and it happens only if we have given to God some quiet time and undivided attention.

How many of you have ever made a retreat? How made of you have made a day of recollection? Recollection means "gathering in." A time of recollection is a time to gather ourselves in, to concentrate on what is most important in our life, to open our mind and heart to the wonder of God in us and in our world. We can do this alone or with others. A group day of recollection will include presentations, communal prayer, and time for silent meditation and personal prayer.

We will have an opportunity for such a day soon. How many of you will come? How much time are you willing to set aside to nourish your faith in Jesus Christ and your life of union with God, to "acquire a fresh, spiritual way of thinking"?

The imperative is clear: "You must put on that new self, created in God's image, whose justice and holiness are born of truth" (Ephesians 4:24). The promise is all we can ever want. Jesus says: "I am the bread of life. No one who comes to me shall ever be hungry, no one who believes in me shall thirst again" (John 6:35).[38]

The Light That Shines

TIME: AUGUST 6, 1989
SEASON: THE TRANSFIGURATION OF THE LORD (YEAR C)
SCRIPTURE READINGS: DANIEL 7:9–10, 13–14;
    2 PETER 1:16–19; LUKE 9:28–36

The story of the Transfiguration of Jesus on a mountain in Galilee before three of his disciples may seem to us like something that took place long ago and far away, something belonging to a different world, a different mentality. Does it have anything to say to us today? Do we have any similar experiences that might help us understand what the Scripture readings are trying to communicate?

We certainly have a similar need. All three readings, all three references to visions of glory are intended to give hope, comfort, reassurance. The first reading from the book of Daniel was addressed to the Jews who were suffering under the persecution of the Greek King Antiochus IV: they are told that God's kingdom will prevail in the end. The Gospel stories of the Transfiguration are all placed between the first and the second prediction of the passion by Jesus and his invitation to the disciples to take up their cross and follow him. The Transfiguration is a glimpse and an anticipation of the Resurrection to reassure them that the cross will be transformed in brilliant glory.

The second reading is addressed to Christians at the beginning of the second century after Christ. They were weary of persecution and suffering, bewildered by the troubling delay of the long-awaited Second Coming of the Lord. The writer reminds them of the memory of the Transfiguration and Resurrection and tells those who doubt and whose faith is shaken that the Risen Lord is already reigning now, and that he will return. They are to wait with patience, as one waits for the dawn to appear and the morning star to rise.

Where do we go to meet the glory and the promise of God? Where do we go for hope and reassurance?

On this date, August 6, 1945, at 8:15 in the morning there was a brilliant flash of light, as dazzling as the sun, in the sky

over Hiroshima, and an ominous cloud rose to the sky, the
mushroom cloud of the first atomic bomb that killed 100,000
people. The atomic age had begun, and it has profoundly transfigured the shape of human history. A moment of revelation
of the power of evil, of the power to destroy.

  I would like to read you a poem by Martha Keys Barker,
titled "Transfiguration."

  Behold Nagasaki, Hiroshima
  their mountains splendid
  with atomic fire
  their people transfigured
  by atomic blast
  their survivors
  writhing in the valley
  begging some splendid Christ
  to touch and make whole.
  Behold the radiant Bomb:
  defying the law
  ignoring the prophets.
  Behold, o man
  and be struck dumb
  by unspeakable terror.
  Feast
  of Disfiguration
  born not of the mountain's vision
  but of dumb demons
  refusing to see in other—
  sister and brother
  seeing only enemy
  building always walls
  to keep the other out . . .
  "Now there are only two ways to walk;
  Toward the radiance of the transfigured Christ
  or the radiance of the Bomb."
  . . . .
  toward the radiance that glorifies,
  or the radiance that vaporizes.
  "This day I set before you life and death,
  a blessing and a curse;
  Choose this day whom you will serve."[36]

Death need not be the last word on human history: this is the message of the death and resurrection of Jesus, anticipated in the Transfiguration. We have God's word of promise and reassurance. We hear this word proclaimed in the liturgy, we read it in the Scriptures. Do we keep it alive in our memory and in our life?

Roger Williams lived with the Wampanoag Indians during the winter before he founded Providence, Rhode Island.

> One day he found several members of the tribe sitting on a bluff overlooking the river and the setting sun. As the glorious colors of the sunset deepened about them, the men and women gently rocked back and forth repeating the phrase 'Ku Manitou, Ku Manitou,' a phrase that we would translate as 'There is God.' . . . Roger Williams recounts two other times when he heard the phrase. Once, during a winter storm when the wind rocked the small huts and howled in the trees outside, the Wampanoags sat in their huts around their fires, gently rocking and repeating 'Ku Manitou.' Another time, when one member of the tribe had fallen through the ice, some members began to form a human chain, lying down on the ice to reach the struggling man. The remainder of the tribe sat on the shore watching the rescue and repeating, 'Ku Manitou, Ku Manitou—There is God. There is God.'[37]

God does break through in our life, now and again. We may not be anxious to recognize his presence, because it often challenges us to change and be transformed, to reflect his light in our world. But it is only in our faith that we can keep alive the hope that Jesus' death and resurrection has transfigured the face of history. It is only through our living memory of Jesus' faithful life, suffering, death, and resurrection that we can keep hope that the final flash of light will signal the salvation and not the destruction of humanity.

But this faith and hope engage our life; they call us to live a life patterned after Jesus' own life and journey to Jerusalem. We come to meet the Lord on the mountain as we celebrate his death and resurrection in the Eucharist. We come down the mountain and return to the world to make him present there and to transfigure the whole of creation in his power.

Enough, Already!

TIME: AUGUST 8, 1982

SEASON: NINETEENTH SUNDAY IN ORDINARY TIME

SCRIPTURE READINGS: 1 KINGS 19:4–8; EPHESIANS 4:30–5:2;
  JOHN 6:41–51

Have you ever felt like the prophet Elijah in today's reading? "He prayed for death: 'This is enough, O Lord! Take my life for I am no better than my father.'" Elijah is fleeing for his life, trying to hide in the desert. He has triumphed over the prophets of Baal, the local deity, through the ordeal on Mount Carmel, and he killed four hundred of Baal's prophets. Jezebel, the queen who brought the prophets of Baal to Israel, is furious and has sworn to kill Elijah. Elijah's physical, emotional and spiritual exhaustion is brought to a climax in the desert, where the prophet asks for relief in death.

Lord, I have had enough. I can't take any more. Have you ever had this kind of thought? I have felt this way, and truthfully I cannot say that my trials and tribulations have been so overwhelming, or my problems and burdens so unbearable. This leads me to think that other people may experience this same feeling of being exhausted, hopeless, broken.

I was struck by the signs and expressions of fear, hopelessness, despair that I met in Italy. People are putting armored doors on their homes. I saw one house where the locks on the front door were the same type one finds on bank vaults. People talk constantly about how to survive, how to protect themselves. They expect that their personal and national situation will only get worse. They see no hope for the civilized world. Life becomes such a heavy burden, a seemingly impossible task, nothing but struggle day after day. And people ask: Is this kind of life worth living? Why go on? What's the purpose?

As people go on living anyway, because they feel they have no other choice, they isolate themselves more and more. They close in on themselves so they will not be hurt more. They build walls, and bolt their doors, and refuse to answer the doorbell or the knock on the door to minimize risk. (There was a brief respite and a radical change of mood, however, when Italy won the World Cup in soccer!).

Is there a Christian answer? Is there an answer for us? We are told to trust in the gracious love and saving power of God. For Elijah, this meant the divine presence, bread and water, nourishment, a call to continue the journey. At the end of the journey, God will reveal himself in the whisper of a gentle breeze and send Elijah back to face his enemies, to continue his mission. Elijah's bread has become for us a powerful image, a type of the Eucharistic bread given to us for our journey.

But the Gospel does not speak of the Eucharistic bread. Only the last verse of today's reading makes the transition from the discourse on faith in Jesus to the bread that is his flesh for the life of the world. Faith in Jesus Christ: Do we believe in him? Does our faith affect our everyday life? Does it give meaning to all that we do and all that we suffer? Does it make us different persons?

Our faith is not just intellectual assent to a proposition, to a doctrine, but trust, surrender, relationship to a person. When we say to a little child, come to me, we hold out our hands and our arms, as Jesus does to us. Our faith in Jesus is not abstract theological discussion, but personal conviction. We don't simply believe that Jesus is divine, that he knows all things and can do all things, but that in him a loving God has shared our life, that in him that God of power and majesty has revealed himself as someone who cares for us with an immense love.

There is hope, there is meaning, there is purpose in Jesus' life and so also in ours, because we are part of him. If we are part of his body, our thorns are truly his thorns. Our faith is a profound conviction and trust that God will not let us down, that whatever happens to us will not be wasted, that what we are as persons is precious to God and he will not let go of us, will not let evil prevail in our individual lives, in our human history.

This kind of faith is not an escape. Elijah must return to face his enemies, and Jesus cannot escape his own agony. We have to take responsibility for our own lives; we can't just leave everything up to God. This kind of faith is a way of seeing and being that lets us feel God's presence within us and gives us comfort and courage to do what we have to do. "No one can come to me unless the Father who sent me draws him." "No one comes to the Father except through me." The Father leads us to know his Son. In the Son we come to know the love of the Father.

Why did God call us to faith in his Son? Billions of people do not receive that call, and yet they are God's children, too. This call is a unique gift from the mysterious freedom and love of God. All share in the love and care of the Father, but we are privileged to know it, to know him in Jesus Christ. What gratitude we should feel and express in praise and thanksgiving. This special choice, this call to faith, is not for our privilege but for our responsibility, to be instruments of God's salvation for the world, to be signs of his covenant love and compassionate kindness.

We come in faith, we are enriched by the Lord's word and life. We are nourished by his body and blood. We are sent forth to live in faith, to give hope and overcome despair, to banish fear and renew confidence and trust. Come to me all you who labor and are burdened, and I will give you rest.

Receive the Bread of Life

TIME: AUGUST 18, 1991
SEASON: TWENTIETH SUNDAY IN ORDINARY TIME
SCRIPTURE READINGS: PROVERBS 9:1–6; EPHESIANS 5:15–20;
  JOHN 6:51–58

Father Raymond Brown, in his classic commentary on the Gospel of John written for the Anchor Bible series twenty-five years ago, writes: "[W]hile the Synoptic Gospels record the institution of the Eucharist, it is John who explains what the Eucharist does for the Christian."[39] I went back to read Fr. Brown's commentary on these verses. It is difficult reading, and the details are so minute as to be overwhelming, but when one is finished the text acquires extraordinary beauty because of Brown's marvelous insights. I felt I understood much better the power and the depth of these Gospel words. I would like to share some of these insights with you today.

Brown's hypothesis is that the backbone of verses 51–58, which we heard today, "is made up of material from the Johannine narrative of the institution of the Eucharist which originally was located in the Last Supper scene, and that material has been recast into a duplicate of the Bread of Life Discourse"[40] (which we read on the previous two Sundays). What Brown is saying is this: There were several editions of the Gospel in its development to the form we have today. In an earlier draft, there probably was a full description of what Jesus did at the Last Supper. In a later reworking, that material was moved to the place it stands now, and was rewritten to parallel the words of Jesus that speak of him as the bread come down from heaven, that call for belief and acceptance of him as the one whom the Father has sent.

By making this change, the final editor of the Gospel has produced a marvelous juxtaposition of Jesus' twofold presence to believers, as understood by the Johannine community: Jesus' presence in the preached word, and Jesus' presence in the sacrament of the Eucharist.

The whole Church has inherited that twofold structure in its worship, and that sense of Jesus' twofold presence. It is the

structural skeleton of the Divine Liturgy of Eastern Orthodox Christianity, of our Roman Mass, and of all the liturgical
services of Protestant churches that still use the basic structure of the Roman Mass.

There is no doubt that in these verses the sacrament of
the Eucharist comes to the fore and becomes the exclusive
theme:

> No longer are we told that eternal life is the result of believing
> in Jesus; it comes from feeding on his flesh and drinking his
> blood. The Father's role in bringing men to Jesus or giving
> them to him is no longer in the limelight; Jesus himself
> dominates as the agent and source of salvation. Even though
> the verses in 51–58 are remarkably like those of 35–50, a new
> vocabulary runs through them: 'eat,' 'feed,' 'drink,' 'flesh,'
> 'blood.'[41]

The language is realistic, strong, even crude. The stress is
on eating; the phrase actually means "feeding on." In the Bible
the phrase "to eat someone's flesh" is used for hostile action,
for doing harm, and the drinking of blood was looked upon as
a horrendous action forbidden by God. These images cannot
possibly be a metaphor for believing in Jesus, for coming close
to him as disciples. The only positive meaning possible for
these words is as a reference to the Eucharist, and the phrase
in verse 51— "The bread that I shall give is my flesh for the
life of the world"—may be closer to Aramaic words used by
Jesus at the Last Supper than the Eucharistic formula we find
in the Synoptic Gospels.

The Hebrew idiom "flesh and blood" means the whole
human being. Jesus is giving his whole self to be our life, the
life of the world, first by his death on the cross and then by the
memorial celebration of his saving sacrifice in the Eucharist.

We can easily see how a violent argument would arise as
people try to grasp what Jesus has said, try to interpret his
words in different ways. We still have disagreements among
different Christian denominations over the meaning of those
words. The Gospel of John may well reflect the dispute going
on in the evangelist's own time, for the Jewish apologists who
spoke out against Christianity did attack the Eucharist. "[T]he
Fourth Gospel makes no concession to Jewish sensibilities and

insists stubbornly on the reality of the flesh and blood," without, however, going "to the other extreme of attributing magical power to the reception of the flesh and blood of Jesus" as if the Eucharist were similar to the pagan mystery rites of the time.[42]

The verses we are discussing must be understood in the context of the preceding verses, which insist on the necessity of belief in Jesus. When we take the discourse as a whole we see that the gift of life that is given by Jesus comes through "believing" and "eating," or through a believing reception of the sacrament.

What can we expect from this believing participation in the Eucharist? A close, intimate communion with Jesus that brings eternal life. That is how the Gospel of John understands what the Eucharist does for the Christian. Through the Eucharist Jesus remains in the Christian and the Christian remains in Jesus. It is not so much that the food lasts forever, but that the life it produces and nourishes is eternal. And life in communion with Jesus is a participation in the intimate communion that exists between Father and Son.

In the Christian Scriptures there is no more forceful expression of the tremendous claim that Jesus gives us a share in God's own life than verse 57: "Just as the Father who has life sent me, and I have life because of the Father, so the one who feeds on me will have life because of me." We are given the same life that Jesus shares with the Father.

What a rich, incredible treasure we have in the Eucharist! What a tremendous mystery this is, in which we are called to participate every time we approach the table of the Lord! For me, and I am sure for you and for the great majority of Catholic Christians, it is difficult to imagine our worship experience, our spiritual life, our relationship with God, without the Eucharist. In so many ways, the Eucharist is truly the focal point and the crowning event of all that we do and all that we believe.

But we must also constantly ask ourselves how we celebrate the Eucharist. Do we come to the celebration with a heart full of faith and joy and love? Do we participate in the ritual so that we are truly part of this living mystery? Do we approach the hearing of the word and the breaking of the bread with profound respect, reverence, and awe, because we have entered into the very presence of God to share in his life? Is the eating of the bread and the drinking of the cup truly a moment of intimate communion, of life-sharing with the Lord? For, indeed, this is the bread that came down from heaven. All who feed on it shall live forever.

Celebrating the Covenant

TIME: AUGUST 25, 1991
SEASON: TWENTY-FIRST SUNDAY IN ORDINARY TIME
SCRIPTURE READINGS: JOSHUA 24:1–2A, 15–17, 18B;
    EPHESIANS 5:21–32; JOHN 6:60–69

"This sort of talk is hard to endure! How can anyone take it seriously?" I suspect many of you feel this way, but about the words of Paul in the second reading rather than about the words of Jesus about believing in him and eating his flesh and drinking his blood. Today's readings are both beautiful and difficult (especially that second one!). They raise a number of complex issues that are rather critical for our understanding of our faith experience and of our relationships both with one another and with God.

Perhaps we can use the idea of covenant as a theme to give some unity to our reflection. In the first reading we are given excerpts from "the crucial story of the gathering at Shechem, one of the oldest traditions about the coming together of the tribes into the nation of Israel."[43] The story centers around the renewal of the covenant between the people and God, which may have been a yearly ceremony in ancient Israel. In the full text, Joshua recalls for the people what God has done for them, warns them of the adversities they will have to overcome to remain united with God through the covenant, and then asks them to decide for themselves, for the covenant is the result of free choice on both sides.

But this is not only a covenant between the people and God. It is also an agreement among the people themselves, to unite themselves and to become one nation. James Sanders has described this event as "a summit conference of the various victorious groups who . . . had wrested control of significant portions of Palestine from the old Canaanite city-state kingdoms."[44] The groups may have shared an ancient common ancestry, but the basis for their political and social union was a religious one. Shechem was the place where Abraham had first settled, and the promise of the land, made here, is fulfilled at Shechem by the coming together of the tribes to take possession of it. Here everyone pledges allegiance to Yahweh, and this allegiance is what unites the disparate elements. The divine covenant always has a human dimension.

Look at the second reading. Paul takes the marriage relationship as it existed in his time and uses it as a metaphor of the covenant between God and his people that has just been renewed by Jesus' death and resurrection, by which he gained for himself a holy people, a glorious church, holy and immaculate. In making this parallel, Paul calls for a radical transformation of the marriage relationship: It is intended to be a holy covenant, reflecting God's covenant with his people.

We have to try to set aside the words in the passage that we may find offensive and difficult in order to hear what Paul is really saying. He cannot change the marriage institution in the Greco-Roman world of the first century, but he can ask the Christians in that world to live in a radically different way. The key phrase is the opening statement: "Defer to one another out of reverence for Christ." The literal translation is more like, "Be subordinate to one another, obey one another, regard another as higher than oneself."

Two things are clear from the context. In the first place, this is not a one-way street for the wife, the child, the slave, the powerless ones. No. The husband, the father, the master, the one with all the power, is called to subordinate himself, to obey, to regard the powerless one as higher than himself. Second, the model for this behavior is the person and the way of Jesus who, being Lord, freely abased and subordinated himself out of love for us. The marriage covenant, then, is one of mutual, self-giving love and service.

The moment of decision about the covenant relationship with God, proposed by Joshua, is repeated in the Gospel reading. Jesus asks his disciples: "Do you want to leave me, too?" Today's verses connect with the first part of the discourse on the Bread of Life, where the emphasis is on coming to Jesus and believing in him. But, according to the way the chapter is constructed, coming to Jesus and believing in him also involves eating his flesh and drinking his blood, being part of the Eucharistic memorial of the new covenant established in the death and resurrection of Jesus.

"Do you want to leave me, too?" the Lord asks us. I hope our answer is the one of Peter: "Lord, to whom shall we go? You have the words of eternal life. We have come to believe; we are convinced that you are God's holy one." Are we also convinced that believing in Jesus and sharing his bread of life must color and inform all our covenants and covenant relationships? I refer to the covenant that, as in the case of the Hebrew tribes, binds us together as a religious community, a community of faith in Jesus Christ and of love modeled after his sacrificial love. And I also refer to the covenant of marriage. One commentator put it well:

> There are few areas of human life in need of such constant renewal as the habitual modes of male-female relationships, both within and outside of marriage. Precisely because they are grounded in nature itself, they constitute the basis upon which the graced life is built in families, in communities and in society itself. But, for the longest time, despite the strongly christological model of mutual service which Ephesians sought to establish, the way men and women related has been decided almost totally by the culture in which Christians have resided.[45]

A couple of years ago I suggested that sometimes we approach the Eucharist the way we approach food in our culture, through fast food outlets and convenience stores. Maybe we do the same with all our relationships. We run in and run out; we order what we want and we expect to get it right now without any effort on our part, without even getting out of our car. It is a totally impersonal event. There is no connection with the person who cooks the food or who hands it to us, and we often eat it alone, absorbed in our own selves.

Occasionally people will tell me that they have found a priest who can say Mass in fifteen minutes (with the implication that maybe I could speed up my act!), and people at times are unhappy because our liturgies run over forty-five minutes. By way of contrast, think of going to a farmers market, where you get to know the people who grow and sell the food. Taking that food home and slowly, carefully, lovingly cooking a delicious meal, you anticipate the pleasure and delight of the people who will enjoy eating it.

Think of the experience of a leisurely, festive meal, when no one is in a hurry and people enjoy talking and listening to one another, where the sharing of the food truly becomes a symbol of the bonds of family and friendship that bring the people together, where everyone contributes and everyone helps and works together.

Now think of the way you approach your Sunday Eucharist, your prayer and worship, your marriage relationship, your family commitment, your friendships, your covenant community gathered here in the name of Jesus. What is the model that best describes your approach to life and relationships? Is it McDonalds' golden arches or family and friends gathered around a festive table for a special celebration? I hope our life is not all fast food and convenience stores!

Living by the Law

Times: September 1, 1985
Seasons: Twenty-second Sunday in Ordinary Time
Scripture Readings: Deuteronomy 4:1–2, 6–8;
James 1:17–18, 21b–22, 27; Mark 7:1–8, 14–15, 21–23

The issues raised by the biblical readings today are so deep, critical, and of such enormous consequence, that they could keep us talking for months and years on end. But even if we did, we would never be finished, because the issues would change, perhaps, but would never go away. It is the question of human and divine laws, God's commandments and human traditions, external rituals and forms and true religion.

The book of Deuteronomy was written in its present form during the seventh century before Christ, many centuries after the death of Moses. Deuteronomy means "second law." The book is structured as three sermons or speeches of Moses, as if Moses were again promulgating the Law as he had done at Sinai, in the name of Yahweh.

It is much expanded from the original Ten Commandments and contains prescriptions about the temple and its ritual, about ritual purity and purification, about dietary requirements, about a holy way of living. Many of these prescriptions would have had no meaning in the original desert wandering situation when Moses was leading the people to the promised land. They were developed later in an attempt to interpret and apply the Law to a different situation.

Deuteronomy, this second proclamation, second look at the Law, comes at a time of wars and conquest, when the people are scattered, exiled, dispersed, discouraged. The Law is the summary of their history, the expression of their faith response to God's covenant. The Law would become their most precious possession, the one thing that would give them identity, unity, strength—no matter where they were. Deuteronomy becomes the canon, the normative rule of life and worship and faith. It must not be changed, nothing added, nothing subtracted.

Over the centuries, of course, the Law needed to be interpreted, explained, adapted to specific situations. This was the
task of the priests, Levites, and scribes. During the second
century before Christ a group emerged that later would be
known as the Pharisees. They became known as the most faithful observers of the Law. They not only held for a strict, literal
interpretation of the written Law, but also studied and developed oral and written interpretations, traditions, to adapt the
Law to changing social, political, and cultural situations.

By the time of Jesus there were numerous rules and
regulations designed to preserve and protect the purity and
holiness of God's law and teaching, of ritual and worship, of
life and conduct. The rules about purification and ritual
washings mentioned in the gospel reading today belong in
this category. The Pharisees are given a bad press in the Gospels. They appear to be only concerned about this kind of reg-
ulation and not about the true law of God, about external rules
and not about a pure heart.

That is not an accurate picture, although there were exag-
gerations in this direction and misplaced emphasis. This wrong
emphasis is what Jesus spoke against. He did not come to
destroy the Law but to perfect it, to go to the heart of the
Law, to discover its deepest and truest meaning, to look not
only to external behavior but to the deep recesses of the heart, to
what we really are in our deepest convictions and commitments.

What does all this have to do with us today? The issue of
what is God's commandment and what is human tradition,
what is true religion and worship and what is mere external
observance of ritual, has not gone away in two thousand years.
Some current issues include:

✠ Not eating meat on Fridays—denying oneself and
   picking up one's cross, sacrificing for the sake of the
   kingdom and our spiritual growth

✠ The obligation of going to Mass on Sunday—the
   commandment to keep holy the Sabbath; what have we
   done with Sabbath rest?

✠ The question of ordained priests being required not to
   marry, to remain celibate. Is that divine law or human
   precept? Why do we cling to it so desperately?

✠ The question of the ordination of women. The official teaching of the Church tries to argue that its practice is based on divine law. Most theologians and Scripture scholars find little support for that position.

Where do we go from here? Andrew Greeley, speaking recently on National Public Radio, said that American Catholics have become more stubborn, more independent, while remaining loyal to the Church. At one time, people either agreed with everything and followed all the rules, or left the church. Today, they want to remain and be part of the Church, even when they disagree and choose not to obey. People appeal to their own conscience and their personal experience of faith. But that is not all that easy.

Yes, we need to look to our heart, to what we really are. But hear Jesus' warning: "Wicked designs come from the deep recesses of the heart: acts of fornication, theft, murder, adulterous conduct, greed, maliciousness, deceit, sensuality, envy, blasphemy, arrogance, an obtuse spirit. All these evils come from within and render a man impure."

How easy it is to deceive ourselves. How easy it is to appeal to our conscience to justify what we want to do. Yet, ultimately we stand under God's judgment on the basis of our personal, conscientious decisions as to what we see to be right or wrong, just or unjust, good or bad.

But we also need to work hard at forming, developing our conscience according to God's law as perfected by Jesus, according to the spirit of Jesus. We need to work hard to eliminate the evil that is within us so that our conscience may really be a faithful, sincere, reverent response to God's commandments and to the law of Christ.

The second reading suggests another test we can use to see if our religion is true and pure: "Look after orphans and widows in their distress and keeping oneself unspotted by the world make for pure worship without stain before our God and Father." It is this kind of heart and conscience, this kind of religious observance, that we try to bring to our worship of God as we gather for our Eucharistic celebration.

What Does Work Mean to You?

Time: September 4, 1994 (Our Lady of Victory, Fresno)
Season: Twenty-third Sunday in Ordinary Time
Scripture Readings: Isaiah 35:4–7a; James 2:1–5;
    Mark 7:31–37

It may seem somewhat out of place to talk about work on a holiday when everybody wants to forget about work and enjoy a little break from it! But on our national Labor Day holiday, it seems important for us to reflect on the meaning and the role that work plays in our lives as human beings and as Christians. After all, there is no other activity in our lives that takes up as much time and energy as work does.

When I started thinking about today's liturgy I went to pick up a book that by our standards of obsolescence would probably be regarded as outdated, since it was published in 1972. It's a book by Studs Terkel, *Working,* and perhaps some of you remember it. It was a number one best seller for a long time. It's an extraordinary, amazing book that has been used as a textbook for philosophy classes at the university. The author interviewed thousands of people, asking them to talk about what they did, about their work and the meaning of that work for them, as indicated by the book's subtitle: *People talk about what they do all day and how they feel about what they do.*

Today I would like to invite you to imagine that Studs Terkel, or perhaps one of the popular talk show hosts or hostesses, is interviewing you and asking you: "What do you do all day? What kind of work do you do?" How would you answer that question? How would you describe your work activity? But even more important, how would you answer that second question: "How do you feel about what you do all day?"

I suspect your answers would range across the full spectrum of the responses Terkel heard and incorporated in his book. At one extreme is the person for whom work is pure drudgery, something to endure, something whose only redeeming feature is the paycheck at the end of the week, the paycheck that enables the person to live and do whatever he or she feels is really important in life. At the other extreme is the person whose whole life is work, for whom there is nothing else in life, whose whole being and identity is defined almost exclusively by the work they do.

I would hope that most of us fall somewhere in between these extremes, that some of us have, at least some of the time, the ideal that I would describe, at least for myself: being able to have the kind of work that brings me joy and satisfaction, that gives me a sense of accomplishment, that makes me feel that I am doing something worthwhile for myself and for others—but that at the same time does not define my whole life and who I am.

Perhaps even more important for us is to ask what our Christian faith and our Christian traditions have to say about the meaning of work in our life. I want to make two points about that this morning.

The first point is that work is part of the very essence of who we are as human beings and part of our Christian vocation. The second story of Creation in Genesis tells us that God shaped and fashioned the human creature in the garden to cultivate it and to take care of it. From the very beginning, our faith tradition has understood the meaning of our being God's creatures as having the responsibility to take care of God's creation or, even more, to share in God's creative purpose, to continue to work with God in the ongoing process of creation.

If we see work as part of our Christian vocation, then it means that all of us are equally called to give glory to God, to serve God, to help God's kingdom in whatever calling, whatever task we have received, whatever work we do. We are called to live out our Christian faith and calling, to go forth and live out the reality of faith, to grow in our love and union with God, and to witness that faith and hope and love not only at home, but also in our work environments, in all of our tasks. Our daily work, just as much as our daily prayer or our Sunday worship, can give praise and honor to God, if we do it diligently, responsibly, honestly, faithfully, and lovingly.

The second point I would like to make is suggested by today's biblical readings. It seems to me that today's texts have something very powerful to say to us about the meaning of work. We might approach today's readings by asking the question: "What was Jesus' work? What kind of work was Jesus called to do?" In the Gospel, we see Jesus touching the ears and the tongue of a man with a hearing and speech impairment, to enable him to hear and to speak, to listen and to communicate. Jesus calls the man to open himself up to the whole created world around him, and especially to the possibility of human relationships.

I really hear the Gospel suggest that when Jesus says to the deaf man: "Be open," he is not talking just about his ears and mouth. He is addressing himself to the whole person, to the whole human being. He is saying to that person, and to us: "Open up, open yourself to all the ways in which God's revelation and presence is made available to you in the created world and in your fellow human beings."

The healing of the person with the hearing and speech impairment in the Gospel is an echo of the first reading from Isaiah, a typical reading from Isaiah, one of the texts Jesus took and used to define who he was and what he was called to do by the Father. He used the same kind of text in the synagogue when he was handed the scroll of Isaiah and opened it up. He read it and said: "This is being fulfilled in your hearing today." He uses the same kind of text when John the Baptizer sends a couple of disciples to ask him: "What's happening? How come you are not doing the things I said you would do? Are you really the one who is to come, for whom we are waiting, or do we need to look for another? What is going on?"

These are the texts that say that God is coming to save us, to make us well, to make us whole, and the signs of his coming are what we just heard: the blind will see, the deaf will hear, the lame will jump like gazelles, liberty will be announced to the prisoners, and the good news of salvation will be proclaimed first and foremost to the poor. Today's text says that when God comes to save us, all of nature will bloom, even desert and burning sands.

These are signs that the kingdom of God has broken through and is at work in our world and in our history, is at hand for all of us. Jesus is saying: "This is what I have come to do; this is my work." But the incredible mystery is that Jesus, after his resurrection, when he is about to take leave of his disciples, tells them: "Now it is your turn. Now my work will be your work. Now it is up to you to carry on my mission, my task. I entrust it all to you."

As disciples of Jesus, we are called to continue the work that Jesus did, a work from which there is no retirement. (As I prepared this, I wondered how many retired people would be in the congregation. Looking at you, I suspect there are quite a few!) There is no retirement from the call to do Christ's work in the world.

This work calls us to make God's saving mercy and compassion concrete and visible and active in our world here and now, to help people see God's presence in all of creation and in our moment of history. This work calls us to help people hear the word of God and the cry of the poor. Our work as disciples of Jesus calls us to help people speak, to open themselves up to communicate with one another, to understand one another better. The work of discipleship calls us to proclaim the gospel in the full power of its message, in all the beauty of its values; to help people walk with the Lord, and to walk with them as companions in mutual help and support. Our work as disciples of Jesus is to do all that we can to protect our environment so that our earth truly can flourish and bloom.

If we want to hear what James is saying to each of us in the second reading, it is that our work as disciples of Jesus is first to respect each other and to respect other people, not because of the way they look or how they dress or because of what they have; not because they are rich or because they have status in the community; but simply because all of us are children of the same God, all of us are brothers and sisters in the same Lord Jesus Christ. James tells us that, as Christians, we are called to build everywhere profound respect for the dignity of every human being, to share God's special concern for the poor and to be instruments by which God's care and love for the poor is expressed and made present.

That is our work as disciples of Jesus. If this seems daunting or even impossible, let me remind you of the first line from the reading from Isaiah: "Say to those whose hearts are frightened: Be strong, do not be afraid! Our God has come to be with us in his beloved Son, and he has promised to be with us always." That is our comfort and our strength: The Lord is continuing his work in us and with us and through us until the end of time.

Who Do You Say I Am?

TIME: SEPTEMBER 15, 1985
SEASON: TWENTY-FOURTH SUNDAY IN ORDINARY TIME
SCRIPTURE READINGS: ISAIAH 50:5–9A; JAMES 2:14–18;
    MARK 8:27–35

Jesus asks his disciples in today's Gospel reading: "Who do you say that I am?" I don't know of another question more central or more difficult to answer. Who is Jesus for you? What is the meaning of Jesus for your life? I would like to ask you to take a minute of silent reflection to ask the question again and try to answer it for yourself.

I hope you will continue this reflection during the next few days, in your moments of prayer, in the contexts of your daily life. In our readings today, we find several answers to the question. The disciples suggest that Jesus is someone like Elijah, or John the Baptist, a great prophet, a messenger from God. The answer is not wrong, but it is not enough.

Jesus is like the great prophets, Jesus is God's messenger, but in a different way. Peter's answer, "You are the Messiah!" is the right answer, but easily misunderstood. Jesus orders the disciples not to tell anyone, and he corrects their misunderstanding of the meaning of the term. He is Messiah not in power and triumph but in suffering, rejection, death, and resurrection. Peter does not like that answer, but he is told in no uncertain terms how wrong he is.

In the reading from Isaiah, one of what we call the Servant Songs, the way Jesus describes himself is confirmed. The first title given to Jesus by the first believers was that of "servant," based on their interpretation of the figure of the Suffering Servant of Yahweh. They applied this description to Jesus, seeing the servant realized in him.

Whatever Jesus is, whatever his task and mission are, he wants people to be part of it, to be with him and follow him, to be servants as he was, to be willing to let go of their lives as he did. The second reading from the Letter of James spells it out in a very concrete, practical way. Words are not enough.

To say we believe in Jesus is not enough. Faith that does nothing in practice is dead, it has no power to save.

For two thousand years, people have being reflecting on their faith in Jesus and trying to express it in a coherent, systematic way. This is theology. Theologians tell us that Jesus is more than a prophet: He is God himself present among us. Jesus does not just speak God's words, he is the Word made flesh, the personal self-revelation of God. Jesus is Messiah, king, and priest, but his kingdom is not of this world. He brings freedom from sin, the forgiveness of God, eternal salvation for the world. Jesus is human like us in all things except sin. Jesus is God, and in him the fullness of God dwells bodily. Jesus is present among us, in the world, in history, as the Risen Lord. In and through him we meet the living God in the embrace of his love and mercy.

Jesus, the incarnation, God becoming flesh in Jesus of Nazareth, means that "the God who created us, who sustains us, who will judge us, and who will give us eternal life is not a God infinitely removed from us. On the contrary, our God is a God of absolute proximity, a God who is communicated truly in the flesh," in the human reality of Jesus and his followers, in him and through him, "in history, within our human family, and a God who is present in the spiritual depths of our existence as well as in the core of our unfolding human history, as the source of enlightenment and community.[46]

That is what the faith of the Roman Catholic Christian community says about Jesus. But that does not yet answer the question: "Who do you say that I am?" Who do I say Jesus is? The meaning, the reason, the center of my life, when I stop to reflect. It is easy to forget, to become distracted or off center, to head in the wrong direction. Jesus is the model, guide, and leader of my life, even though I don't always follow. Jesus is a friend, companion, lover, even though at times I try to walk alone and forget or lose his presence and fail to love him. Jesus is Lord, for my life belongs to him and is under his rule and his love. Jesus is Savior, for all the promises of peace and joy and justice and right. All my hopes for life and wholeness and richness and fullness, coming to know the mystery of God and being absorbed in and united with the mystery of ultimate love, rest in Jesus Christ.

I learned two phrases of Paul as a very young child, and they have remained with me all my life:

"To me, to live is Christ and to die is gain."

"I live, yet not I but Christ lives in me."

I wish I could say those words about myself and really mean them. Perhaps some day I will. Who do you say Jesus is?

The First Shall Be Last

TIME: SEPTEMBER 22, 1991
SEASON: TWENTY-FIFTH SUNDAY IN ORDINARY TIME
SCRIPTURE READINGS: WISDOM 2:12, 17–20; JAMES 3:16–4:3;
MARK 9:30–37

Can you believe what we have just heard in the Gospel reading? Did you hear what was being said? Did it move from your hearing to your mind and to your heart? The passage is full of incredible and contradictory behavior and ideas. Last Sunday's Gospel reading featured Jesus' first prediction of his suffering, rejection, death, and vindication. In the text of Mark this is followed by the story of the transfiguration of Jesus and the healing of a demon-possessed boy. And now Jesus returns to his grim foreboding about imprisonment, death, and rising from the dead.

He says it so plainly, and the disciples still do not understand, but, remembering Jesus' treatment of Peter in the previous exchange on this subject, they are afraid to open their mouths. Or perhaps *they do not want to understand!* Because, as they are walking along, they are not asking one another what this "rising from the dead" might mean, or how they would feel about the prospect of Jesus being mistreated and put to death. No! They are talking about which one of them is going to be the most important.

They are still thinking of an earthly, triumphant king, and they are debating which one among them would be first, who would hold the position of honor at the right hand of the new king. Can you believe it? No wonder they are embarrassed when Jesus questions them about their conversation on the road!

Patiently, Jesus sits down and gathers the Twelve close to him. This detail suggests that the Gospel of Mark meant this warning for the leaders of the church in a special way. Perhaps the leaders in the community from which this Gospel came were already claiming special privileges and honors. And Jesus tells them: "If anyone wishes to rank first, he must remain the last one of all and the servant of all."

Did you know that in ecclesiastical, church processions the higher the dignity the farther back the person is placed? Perhaps you have noticed that when the pope enters a church or an area for a liturgical celebration he is always last. An ecclesiastical procession goes like this: minor ministers first, followed by deacons, priests, monsignori, special prelates, bishops, archbishops (arranged by seniority of episcopal ordination), cardinals, and pope. I don't know if this Gospel is the reason for this arrangement, but after two thousand years it does not make much difference anyway, for now the last place has become the place of honor, and everyone guards his position carefully. The closer one is to the pope, the higher his rank!

Can we also say "the higher the dignity"? I wonder. If I understand the Gospel correctly, dignity comes from being truly last, like waiting in line to go to the bathroom, or at a check-out stand in the grocery store, and maybe letting someone go ahead of you. And dignity, rank, in the kingdom of God, comes from being willing to be a servant, a servant to everybody, and from being like a child. In the time of Jesus children were totally the property of the father and completely vulnerable; they had no rights, no privileges, no rank, no power. Just like a servant. And we are to be like that! If we accept this ideal we welcome Jesus in our life, and the God who sent him. Can we believe that?

In our society, or in any society for that matter, this does not make sense, does it? Who wants to be last? Why should I want to be last? We are used to a pecking order. I may have to be the servant of somebody and do their bidding, but I also expect someone to take care of my needs, to wait on me, to do my bidding. Isn't that the way things work—in industry, in business, in schools, in politics, in religion, perhaps even in homes? But not in the kingdom of God!

In the kingdom of God we have to make a deliberate choice to be servants to everyone, to renounce power and influence, rank and privilege. The only way we can believe and accept that is if we believe and accept the mystery of God in Jesus Christ, for that is how God revealed himself in him, that is how God acted in him. That is what God became in Jesus: the faithful, suffering servant who is willing to give his life for all, willing to forgo the splendor of divine glory for the limitations of the human condition and the insult of a criminal's death.

The other two readings are a more realistic description of the way things are, the way evil resents and tries to destroy goodness, to put it to the test, because it does not believe that it is real. The second reading describes the roots of evil within the human heart, within us: These are the reasons we have such a hard time believing and accepting the radical demands of discipleship. It is hard to be childlike in a world like ours, to choose to serve others and accept being last, but that is how we enter the mystery of God, because, as one commentator put it:

> The Father of our Lord Jesus Christ, the prodigal Father of a sinful humankind, is the only God we have, the only God there is. The Infant in the manger and the Suffering Servant on the Cross have shown us the truest face of God, the Lord Who rises from the tomb resplendent in His wounds. Take Him or leave Him.[47]

And if we take him, we have to take his word: "If anyone wishes to rank first, he must remain the last one of all and the servant of all."

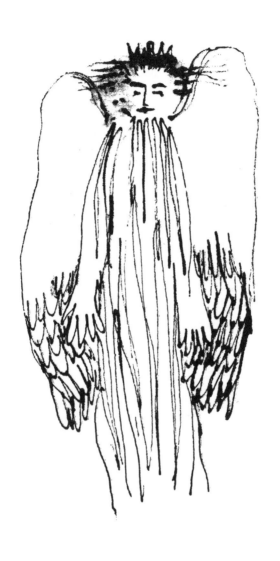

Greatness of Heart

TIME: SEPTEMBER 29, 1985
SEASON: TWENTY-SIXTH SUNDAY IN ORDINARY TIME
SCRIPTURE READINGS: NUMBERS 11:25–29; JAMES 5:1–6;
    MARK 9:38–43, 45, 47–48

There is a very beautiful, expressive word that is not used much any more, but that says so much. The noun is *magnanimity,* the adjective is *magnanimous.* The Latin form is made up of two words: *magnus* and *animus:* great spirit, great mind, great soul—a heart big enough to take in, to welcome, to rejoice in, to incorporate, to draw from, everything and everyone we meet. I think of people such as Mahatma Gandhi, Mother Teresa, Martin Luther King, Helen Keller, as great-spirited people, people of evident magnanimity.

One of my old and revered professors, Dr. Bernard Loomer, has written an article by the title "S-I-Z-E Is the Measure." He states:

> By size I mean the stature of a person's soul, the range and depth of his love, his capacity for relationships. I mean the volume of life you can take into your being and still maintain your integrity and individuality, the intensity and variety of outlook you entertain in the unity of your being without feeling defensive or insecure. I mean the strength of your spirit to encourage others to become freer in the development of their diversity and uniqueness. I mean the power to sustain more complex and enriching tensions. I mean the magnanimity of concern to provide conditions that enable others to increase in stature.[48]

He does not say it explicitly, but I know Dr. Loomer thinks of God that way, and that for him all concepts of God, all ways of speaking and thinking of God, are not big enough. Nothing that we can ever say or think can ever exhaust the mystery of God, the magnanimity, the greatness of the heart of God.

The story in the book of Numbers, our first reading, tells about Eldad and Medad, who had been chosen and invited but for some reason refused to go to the tent. Perhaps they were mad at Moses, or they got the wrong date, the wrong time for the meeting. That does not stop God. His spirit finds them wherever they are and they speak out as ones possessed by God.

Joshua, hearing about this, manifests a smallness of heart, a meanness of spirit. In his view, only those who belong to the inner circle are entitled to prophesy, only those who are with us can share in our privileges. Only those who are on our side, who think as we do, who are loyal to us, who share the same values, are entitled to receive the gift of God, to be touched by him.

Moses' answer speaks of the generosity, the magnanimity of God. In the prophetic word of Joel 2:28–29, God will pour out his spirit on all the people. There is no reason to be exclusive, miserly, jealous, grasping, when it comes to the gifts of God. He gives freely to everyone.

We find the same kind of scene in the Gospel reading. Someone who is not of the company of the disciples is using the name of Jesus and is successful in expelling demons. How does he dare do something like that without authorization? Who gave him permission? What right does he have to exercise the power that Jesus has shared with his disciples? Jesus seems to answer: Don't worry, let him be, rejoice. If evil is being conquered and good is happening, what does it matter who is doing it? He is on our side, he is doing the same thing we want to do.

The family of God's children is not a private club with exclusive membership. The gift of God's love is not limited by our ability to dispense it. The gift of faith in the saving power of our God does not depend on our ability to say the right words, to know the right formula.

That second paragraph of the Gospel reading, about cutting off your hand or your foot, or plucking out your eye, is difficult to take. Some people have read it and turned away in disgust from a God who would ask such things. We can explain the language as Middle Eastern hyperbole, we can make reference to Gehenna as the city dump for Jerusalem, always smoldering with a foul-smelling smoke as the refuse is being burned, but we are still left with the question of hell, of eternal punishment.

Here is where our heart and spirit need to be big enough to take in both the mystery of human freedom and the mystery of God's love and grace. The human heart is free to turn away from God, to reject his love, to choose rebellion and alienation. But I believe that God's heart is big enough to continue to offer his saving love forever, without limits of time and place. I believe that he will save everything worth saving, that his goodness is greater than all our evil, that his love is stronger than all our denials and rejections.

Dr. Loomer concludes the article I mentioned with this story from Elie Wiesel:

> When the great Rabbi Israel Ball Shem-Tov saw misfortune threatening the Jews it was his custom to go into a certain part of the forest to meditate. There he would light a fire, say a special prayer and the miracle would be accomplished and the misfortune averted. Later, when his disciple, the celebrated Mazid of Mezritch, had occasion for the same reason to intercede with heaven, he would go to the same place in the forest and say: 'Master of the universe, listen. I do not know how to light the fire but I am still able to say the prayer!' And the miracle would again be accomplished. Still later, Rabbi Moseh-Leib of Sasov, in order to save his people once more would go into the forest and say: 'I do not know how to light the fire, I do not know the prayer, but I know the place, and this must be sufficient.' It was sufficient and the miracle was accomplished. Then it fell to Rabbi Israel of Rizhyn to overcome misfortune. Sitting in his armchair, his head in his hands, he spoke to God: 'I am unable to light the fire and I do not know the prayer; I cannot even find the place in the forest. All I can do is to tell the story, and this must be sufficient.' And it was sufficient.

Wiesel's and Loomer's conclusion: "God made man because he loves stories."

My conclusion today: It is sufficient because the heart of God is so great that he can accept whatever we have to offer him, because the stature of his spirit, the range and depth of his love, his capacity for relationships, is not limited by our lack of love and poverty of spirit.

Striving for the Ideal

TIME: OCTOBER 3, 1976

SEASON: TWENTY-SEVENTH SUNDAY IN ORDINARY TIME

SCRIPTURE READINGS: GENESIS 2:18–24; HEBREWS 2:9–11;
    MARK 10:2–16

Last Sunday someone asked me how many single-parent families we have registered in the parish. I did not know, but I checked. We have fifteen registered, and I know of several more. And how many people are present here today who have been divorced and remarried? I have no way of knowing. Is there anyone here who does not have one or more friends who have gone through the experience of divorce and who have either remarried or are struggling with the question of remarriage both from the human and the religious perspective?

Is there anyone here who has not either experienced personally or shared with a friend the anguish of coming to the conclusion that a marriage has failed, or the terrible hurt of being suddenly abandoned by the marriage partner, or the sinking feeling that it was all a big mistake from the beginning? For the Catholic, a major factor in the process of reaching the decision of divorce, and in the anguish and the fear for the future that go with that decision, is the question of the person's relationships with God and with the community of the Church.

What has the Church done about this situation? At the official level, not much has happened yet. At the local level of pastoral care there are a variety of approaches and considerable confusion. That is why I feel that the only thing I can do is share my thinking, my reflection, my feelings, at this time. I want to emphasize that I am giving you *my own opinions* and thoughts, *not* the official teaching of the Church.

I think that in this matter the responsibility of the Christian community is twofold. First, to proclaim and to maintain the ideal of Christian marriage, and in every way possible to encourage its members to commit themselves to this ideal, and to help them live as faithfully as possible to the ideal. Second, to work with the greatest of empathy and sympathy, with compassion and understanding, with every person whose marriage has failed to live up to the ideal, so that they can continue to search for human happiness and growth and can be reassured of God's forgiving love, and of the acceptance and care of the Christian community.

Let me restate the ideal of marriage for the Christian, as I understand it. I think it would be a tragic mistake to abandon or to weaken or compromise that ideal simply because it seems to be more and more difficult to live by it. If we were to change the ideal for the sake of all the personal, social, and cultural problems confronting the institution of marriage, we would be unfaithful to the biblical proclamation and to the history of Christian traditions.

Some writers today would argue that this biblical ideal of marriage is culturally conditioned, the product of the culture of ancient Israel, and that it must be changed to fit our culture. They would point to today's first reading, from Genesis, which gives us the second, more male-oriented, account of the creation of man and woman. This selection reflects an age when male domination of women in the domestic circle was taken for granted. That is the reason for the imagery of the woman coming from the man.

Today, women everywhere are pointing out how much they have suffered at men's hands because of the literal acceptance of the ancient categories reflected in this passage. To be sure, marriage and family patterns are subject to cultural change. This causes some to say that the monogamous union, with the assumption of lifetime fidelity "in one body," is but another ancient settlement calculated to continue the subjugation of women by men. Jewish and Christian conjugal morality are stigmatized as comprising an unenlightened religious sanction for domestic tyranny of the worst kind.

But I think there is much more to the cultural phenomena involved both in this passage and in the overall treatment of marriage in both Hebrew and Christian Scriptures. The one, faithful, loving, fruitful union of husband and wife in marriage becomes the most powerful image of God's relationship to his people, thus giving this ideal of marriage a profound religious significance and a foundation in the very mystery of God's relationship to his creation. I believe that much of our culture still accepts and supports this ideal. I know that whenever I have encountered people who were earnestly striving to reach the ideal, with some measure of success, the beauty, the warmth, the depth of their relationship confirmed my conviction that this is a human as well as a Christian ideal.

The Christian ideal of marriage, as I understand it, is a union between a man and a woman that is personal and total, abiding and indissoluble, faithful and loving, fruitful and creative, a union that reflects and signifies, not only for the members of the family but for the whole community, the mysterious reality of the union of God with his people, of the love of Jesus the Christ for his body, the Church.

It is a union in which two persons give themselves to each other completely, in a companionship that the human being cannot experience with any other element of God's creation. It is a union that calls for the greatest possible sharing of thoughts, feelings, and emotions, of mind and heart and body. Please remember that when Genesis speaks of the two becoming one body, one flesh, that the biblical language of "body" and "flesh" means the whole person, the whole human being in its earthly condition.

It is a union that is intended to be for a lifetime. Only death can come to separate husband and wife, and for many, I am sure, even that separation is only for a time; the union will continue into eternity. It is indissoluble because husband and wife are joined together by God, and the bond of their union represents the unending, unbreakable bond between God and his creation.

It is a union that calls for the partners to be faithful to one another, not merely in the sense of sexual exclusivity but also in the sense of being completely for each other, of standing by each other, of putting one's total trust in the other, of being able to always count on the other to be faithful as God is faithful to us, even when we are not faithful to God.

It is a union that is fruitful and creative, not only because of a command to be fruitful and multiply, but because love wants to be creative, because love tends to express itself in the fruit of its act, in the child born of the act of unity and love, just as the human race is the fruit of God's creative love, just as the love of Jesus for his Church is intended to bear fruit in new children of God and members of his family, the family of the beloved Son.

This is the Christian ideal of marriage. As I have described it, it sounds like an impossible ideal. In its perfection, as the image of the love of God and Jesus Christ, it is impossible. But, accepting its human limitations and the possibility of only limited achievement, it is eminently worth striving for. We must believe in it, hope for it, work for it, and grow toward this ideal little by little.

What happens when the ideal becomes even humanly impossible, when a marriage fails, so that there is nothing left but harm and destruction for all involved? The union will be terminated, the people will separate. Traditionally and officially, the Church has accepted separation but has regarded remarriage, after the break-up of a union that was legitimate and sacramental, as a condition of sinfulness that would bar the people from full participation in the life of the Christian community—especially the reception of the sacraments of penance and reconciliation and the Eucharist.

Officially that position has not changed. The only official development has been a new understanding of the kind of maturity and emotional stability necessary for a fully human consent to a lifetime decision such as marriage. Today there are increasing numbers of dissolutions of marriage that are recognized by marriage tribunals in the Church on the basis that inadequate consent made the marriage null and void from the beginning.

Unofficially, in the day-to-day pastoral care of divorced people at the parish level, a number of priests will leave up to the conscience of the individual persons involved the decision as to the degree of participation in the life of the community and the sacramental life of the Church. In other words, if the persons concerned feel in their conscience that they are doing the best they can, given their current situation, if they are convinced that second marriage can be good and acceptable to God, that God has forgiven them for whatever responsibility and sin was involved in the break-up of the first marriage, the priests will respect their sincere conscience and their honest decision, and administer the sacraments to them. This pastoral practice is by no means generally accepted, and it is officially rejected.

At the same time, there is mounting pressure from priests and people, and even from official bodies such as the Canon Law Society of America, for an official change in the attitude and policies of the Church in this matter. In the December 7, 1974 issue of *America* magazine, published by the Jesuits of the United States, there is an article written by Charles M. Whelan, who is an associate editor of the publication as well as a professor in the Law School of Fordham University and a special legal advisor to the U.S. Catholic Conference. The title of the article is "Divorced Catholics: A Proposal," and the proposal is this:

> Catholics who have divorced and remarried should be officially readmitted to full communion in the Church, providing they can satisfy the following four conditions: (1) Their first marriage is irretrievably lost. (2) The present methods of official reconciliation (death of the first spouse; annulment; Pauline and Petrine privileges) are unavailable. (3) The parties to the second marriage have demonstrated by their lives that they have a sincere desire to participate fully in the life of the Church. (4) There are solid grounds for hope that the second marriage, even though it cannot be officially celebrated as yet by the Church, will be in all other respects a Christian marriage.[49]

Not only was this article published in a Catholic magazine, but the editors of this highly respected publication endorsed Whelan's position editorially. The editorial concludes: "The proposal we have endorsed is theologically, spiritually and canonically sound. It holds out hope for a new life for millions of American Catholics. We urge that it be studied, discussed and adopted promptly."[50]

I might want to argue about the conditions, but I am in full agreement with the proposal. It may be necessary for the Church community to decide that this kind of second marriage cannot be celebrated in the church, in order to make that point that it falls short of and fails to live up to the ideal of Christian marriage, as the community understands that ideal. But I do not think that the Church, the Christian community, should look upon remarriage as a permanent condition of sin and continuing separation from the body of Christ, as an insurmountable obstacle to full communion in the Eucharist.

This is not a new idea in Christian history. It has been the practice in Eastern Christianity from ancient times, and it is the practice in the Orthodox Church today.

What, then, of today's Gospel and its condemnation of divorce and remarriage? We must accept it, and I don't think there is any way to soften it. We must see divorce as a failure and remarriage as something less than the ideal. The people who find themselves caught up in this situation must examine themselves to discover whatever sinfulness might be involved. But they also must be encouraged to trust in the merciful love and compassionate forgiveness of God.

I would like to remind you that one of the parallel messages in the Gospel of Matthew, on the question of divorce and remarriage, is found in the context of the Sermon on the Mountain. And I would like to ask you: How many of us live up to the ideal of Christian life proclaimed there? How many of us live by the Beatitudes, day in and day out? How many of us live by the ideal of nonviolence and always turn the other cheek? How many of us will give away our shirt, when someone asks for our coat? How many of us give to everyone who asks, without expecting anything in return? How many of us have never looked at another with lust, or called another a name in anger?

We must admit, if we are honest, that we fail in many, many ways to live up to the radical demands of the ethic of Jesus and of life in the kingdom of God. And yet *we* believe in God's forgiveness and *we* continue to live as members in good standing of the Christian community. Why should the question of divorce and remarriage be treated differently?

A case could be made that the more restrictive laws are necessary to protect and defend the institution of marriage.

But my understanding of the life and ministry of Jesus tells me that persons come first, and that ministry and service in the Church should be for the sake of persons.

That is the reason why I believe that, in this time of crisis for the institution of marriage and the family, the Christian community must not only hold on firmly to the ideal but also must care tenderly for the wounds and nurture lovingly the hopes of the persons who are caught up in the crisis.

This is how I understand the responsibility of the Church today.

The Challenge of Wealth

Time: October 10, 1976

Season: Twenty-eighth Sunday in Ordinary Time

Scripture Readings: Wisdom 7:7–11; Hebrews 4:12–13; Mark 10:17–30

Are there any rich young men or rich young women here today? No? How about a rich old man or a rich old woman? If there are any, be sure to see me right after Mass. We have a couple of projects that need your support. Or maybe I am too late. Maybe you have already decided to sell all that you have and give it to the poor.

I'm not only trying to be facetious, but also trying to point out that there is surely not one person here who would describe himself or herself as being rich. And, of course, if I'm not rich, the Gospel doesn't apply to me, does it? I can go right on and live the way I've always lived and not be bothered.

I don't know about you, but reflecting on today's Gospel I realized and experienced more immediately the meaning of the words of that second reading: "God's word is living and effective, sharper than any two-edged sword. It penetrates and divides soul and spirit, joints and marrow. He judges the reflections and the thoughts of the heart." I feel this sharp edge of God's word, especially when it comes to the question of material possessions and poverty. This is where I feel myself most torn and divided.

If we were shocked and amazed at the words of the Gospel, perhaps we can take consolation in the fact that so were the disciples who heard Jesus speak them for the first time. You can almost hear their thoughts. "What on earth is he saying?" "Where does he come off with this kind of stuff?" They were not rich men, either, but what they heard from Jesus was the direct opposite of what they had learned from the rabbis, from the scriptures.

From those sources came the idea that to be rich and powerful and to have great responsibilities is a sign that the person has found favor with God. In contrast, it was believed, to be poor was a sign of God's rejection or punishment. I think we still have some of that kind of feeling in our church and society today. In the time of Jesus, observance of the Law worked to favor the rich. They were the ones who had the time and the means and the leisure to abide by all the ceremonial practices and social responsibilities imposed by the Law. The poor spent all their time and energy simply trying to survive. So how could Jesus say what he said?

It is hard to know what was going through the mind of that rich young man. It is hard to know exactly what he was being asked to do. All we know is that he went away sad because he was unable to accept the Lord's challenge. Maybe he was asked to let go of all his earthly goods, but I think it would be wrong to construe the gospel to say that we must reject all the goods of this earth.

There is nowhere in the Gospel that I know where riches in themselves are declared evil. Nor were riches corrupting to this young man. He was a good man. He had kept all the commandments. That's saying something! He was a righteous and good person. He was asked, however, to go a step farther, to commit himself not only to saving himself and gaining eternal life, but to follow Jesus, to become a disciple. At that point, at least for him, wealth became an obstacle.

What is the challenge of the Gospel for us today? I would like to raise three questions.

First, in what do we ultimately put our trust? In money, investments, property, possessions? Are these the things on which we rely for status, for power, for security, for the enjoyment of a good and full life? Or are we willing to put our trust in God, to rely on God as the sole source of our security and well-being?

Tennessee Williams, in the play *Cat on a Hot Tin Roof,* provides similar commentary on the rich, during the climactic dialogue between Big Daddy, a wealthy southern Plantation owner, and Brick, his favorite son, a former football hero now turned alcoholic. Big Daddy has just come home from a clinic and believes he has been given a clean bill of health, while everybody else knows that he is dying from cancer. This is what he was afraid of, but he has not been told. And now he reflects on his fear, on the fear of death and on the relief he felt when he was told that all he had was a "spastic colon." He says to Brick, "The human animal is a beast that dies and if he's got money, he buys and buys and buys. And I think the reason he buys everything he can is that in the back of his mind he has the crazy hope that one of his purchases will be everlasting life, but that can never be, can never be."

I am sure you understand what I am trying to say. I am not saying that trust in God means that we can sit back, stop working and wait for God to take care of us. I think we need to ask ourselves: In that moment of fear and uncertainty, when we begin to wonder about the future and about what life has in store for us, and we are afraid, what do we think of first? Of how much money we have in the bank, or of the assurance of God's love and care?

The second question: How far are we willing to go in the following of Jesus? What are we willing to give up, to let go, if it interferes or conflicts with our call to discipleship to Jesus Christ? We want to follow Jesus, I'm sure. We call ourselves disciples, we call Jesus "Lord." We have all tried to go beyond the commandments in living a Christian life. Has it cost us anything? Has it made any demands on us? Would we be willing to leave home, brothers and sisters, mother and father, children and property, for Jesus and for the gospel?

Actually, it is difficult to know what we would be willing to give up until we are actually faced with the choice, until the time we are really confronted with the need to choose one or the other. But I think the Gospel says at least this: The disciples of Jesus must be prepared, must at least be willing, to leave everything behind and to give up everything, if and when the time comes that this is what they are asked to do, this is the only choice left. I can understand how we might continue to pray that that day never comes. But if it does come, if the day comes when we can no longer keep in balance our nice, comfortable, pleasant life with the demands of the gospel and of discipleship, what choice will we make?

And the third question: Are we willing to share what we have with the poor? We all have something. By comparison with the rest, the great majority of people in the world, we are rich.

There is a story in the Talmud that tells of the conversion of the rich man. The rich man was a rabbi. Although he was very wealthy and very knowledgeable, he was not very charitable. The great Rabbi Akiba came to him with an offer he couldn't refuse. He said he could buy for him an entire village and that it would be a very good investment. So the rich man gave Akiba the money for the purchase and Akiba went out and gave all the money to the poor in the village. When the rich man asked Akiba for the deed to his newly acquired property, Akiba opened the book of Psalms and read: "He has scattered abroad. He has given to the needy. His righteousness endures forever." "This is what I have purchased for you," said Akiba. The rich man understood and embraced him.

Are we willing to share our material possessions? Not so much for the sake of our own righteousness, but for the sake of the brother and sister in need? Not because it is a good investment, but because a man, woman, or child needs our help?

That is why I think the word of God cuts deep, like a double-edged sword. But, like the surgeon's knife, the word of God can also bring healing, health, wholeness, new being, new freedom to our life. That is why we must listen carefully, hear what is deep within us, and reflect, pray, and answer.

Why Do We Suffer?

TIME: OCTOBER 16, 1994 (OUR LADY OF VICTORY, FRESNO)
SEASON: TWENTY-NINTH SUNDAY IN ORDINARY TIME
SCRIPTURE READINGS: ISAIAH 53:10–11; HEBREWS 4:14–16;
MARK 10:35–45

Humility, obedience, suffering, a bath of pain, being crushed in infirmity. I ask you: What kind of a program is that? It is the program for a life of discipleship of Jesus Christ. No wonder Jesus had so few disciples! It's a wonder that anyone at all would follow him once they heard what Jesus was saying and asking of them. Mark's explanation is that the disciples never understood what Jesus was saying and what Jesus was calling them to be and to do. In today's Gospel, we have a very clear example of the kind of misunderstanding that Mark attributes to the disciples over and over again in his Gospel.

In the context of today's passage, Jesus had just finished telling his disciples, for the third time, that his destiny in Jerusalem was suffering and death. He just finishes saying that, and what happens? Two of the disciples, James and John, come right up to him and say: "Hey, Lord! We want you to do something for us. We want to be seated one at your right hand and one at your left hand when you come into your kingdom." What they are expecting is an earthly kingdom that would revive and renew the glories of the kingdom of David, and they want a position of power when that happens.

Jesus' response to them is a question: "Can you drink my cup of suffering? Can you share my pain?" The other disciples are very upset because they feel James and John are trying to put one over on them. Jesus gathers all of the disciples and tells them: "If you want to be my follower you have to become a servant." What Jesus says is much more dramatic than that: "You have to become like a slave, a slave! And you have to serve the needs of all."

What does this say to us today? We are called to be disciples of Jesus Christ, aren't we? Do we understand what we are being asked? Are we willing to follow Jesus, to accept the call to discipleship? It is a call to be servants, to be slaves to the needs of others. Do we understand that the discipleship of Jesus Christ means participation in the redemptive suffering of the Lord?

Let's look at that for a moment. What does redemptive suffering mean? Is it just some kind of sugar coating on the whole idea of pain and suffering, to make us feel good and stop asking questions about it? We used to say "Offer it up." Did that make the pain go away? Did it make us feel better? Is suffering some kind of divine invention for the human creature? Is the fact that we suffer part of God's plan for us? Frankly, I don't think so.

I think pain and suffering, evil and darkness, are the inescapable conditions of our material world. We have pain and suffering because our material world breaks down. If someone is involved in a serious automobile accident, it is not just the car that breaks down; our body does, too. And, just like everything else, our body grows old and grows weaker, it wears out and breaks down.

And there is freedom in the world, and freedom means that people can do crazy things—drive-by shootings, abusing children, using violence as a means of acquiring power and possessions. Evil and suffering are the result of the limitations of our material world and the aberrations of our human freedom.

What happens in the mystery of the death and resurrection of Jesus is that God reveals his power to take pain, suffering, and even death, and transform them into something with value, to give them meaning and a power for good. Because of the death and the resurrection of Jesus, the Easter mystery we celebrate again today in this Eucharist, we know that even suffering, pain, desolation, the loss of everything, even death, are not a total waste. There is something good that can come out of our pain and suffering. There is goodness that can come out of evil and darkness.

We also heard that in the first reading, a very brief excerpt from one of the beautiful songs of the Suffering Servant in the book of the prophet Isaiah. There we heard that through his suffering the servant shall justify many. The servant was Israel in exile, and the servant is Jesus dying on the cross, the Jesus who said that he came not to be served but to serve, and to give his life in ransom for "the many," for all.

We are part of that transforming reality that the power of God brings to bear on the mystery of evil. Paul, writing to the Colossians, says: "I now rejoice in my suffering for your sake, and in my flesh I am completing what is lacking in Christ's afflictions for the sake of his body, that is the church" (1:24). In our suffering, in our flesh, we are called to complete Christ's afflictions for the sake of the salvation of the world. How can we think that evil, pain, and suffering have no meaning when we see them from that perspective?

But even from our human experience, how can we ever think that the heart-breaking pain of a mother who sees her child killed by a bullet has no meaning, no value? How can we imagine that what is happening to our children, all the violence and abuse that is inflicted on them, has no meaning, no power? It must have the power to move our hearts and minds to find answers and solutions to the problem of senseless and random violence that plagues our cities. How can we imagine that the pain and devastation of a human body suffering through the process of cancer or another degenerative disease has no meaning, no value, is nothing but a waste? I cannot believe that is the case. That is not what comes out of my faith in the mystery of Christ.

Think of your own experiences with pain and suffering. See if your experiences support what I am trying to say, namely, that pain and suffering, even from our human perspective, can help us to grow, mature, become better persons. Why does it work that way? Why does it have to be that way? I don't know, but I do know that we learn through pain and suffering.

We learn our limits: We learn that we can't do everything and we can't have everything. We learn our need for God. Our material world will never be enough to satisfy all our desires and all our needs. Only God can do that.

We learn compassion: If we are able to be in touch with the reality of our own suffering, we will become much more compassionate toward someone else who is suffering. How many times have you seen that pain and suffering in a family or in a relationship helps people to discover both how much they love and how much they are loved, to discover the tremendous power of love that is in us?

Pain and suffering can bring out the hidden depths of goodness in us and in others, can bring about profound change in us, can help us discover the hidden sources of strength that are in us. I hope that you can think of some concrete experiences that support what I am staying.

I would like to share with you the story of a good friend who for twelve or more years was called upon to care for his wife, who suffered from a degenerative disease. Eventually it came to the point where she was totally immobile, with no recognition or response. The love, the tenderness with which this man took care of his wife was an inspiration to many people and to me, personally. His example made a difference in my own ministry. About a year after his wife died, my friend died as well. He had been battling with cancer and, once his work of caring for his wife was done, he simply let go and died.

I could tell you much more about this man and his loving service, but I want to share with you a television program I watched on which one segment told the story of Nicholas Green, the eleven-year-old boy who was killed in a hold-up attempt on a highway in Southern Italy. Perhaps you saw the program, and even if you did not, I am sure you know the story, because it has made headlines all over the Western world. When you reflect on what happened, it looks like a senseless, totally meaningless tragedy. A car comes by and its occupants start shooting at another car, when the driver refuses to pull over and be robbed. A young boy is hit in the head by a bullet, and all attempts to save him fail.

The decision of his parents to donate the organs of their young son, whose life full of promise had been cut short so brutally, so that other people could live, has touched people all over the world. A week ago I called my sister, who lives in Italy, and the first thing she said to me was: "Have you heard the story of this boy and his family?" During this short time, in Italy alone, organ donations have increased more than 400 percent. Just imagine what that has done in terms of helping people to live. The death of that one boy has brought life to hundreds of other people.

This is the message of the Easter mystery: not that pain and evil are done away with, but that they have been given meaning because God in Jesus Christ has shared our pain and the suffering of our world. And the God who entered our history in the person of Jesus Christ is still with us, suffering with us, struggling with us, and will not let our pain go to waste. I don't think that God in Jesus Christ calls us to suffer for the sake of suffering. God calls us to be disciples of his beloved son. And Jesus calls us to be his followers, even if his destiny is suffering, because to be a servant often leads to rejection, to persecution, to suffering.

God in Jesus Christ has called us to work with him to bring something good and worthwhile out of evil and darkness, out of pain and suffering. God has called us to be instruments of his compassion and loving care to our suffering world.

Freedom and Responsibility

Time: October 28, 1973
Season: Thirtieth Sunday in Ordinary Time
Scripture Readings: Jeremiah 31:7–9; Hebrews 5:1–6;
     Mark 10:46–52

Show me the way to go home." Are we willing to say this, to ask and mean it? For a while it seemed that the prevailing attitude might have been expressed best as: "Get out of my way so that I can do my own thing." I don't hear this phrase much anymore, but I don't know if that is because of a change in attitude or because everybody is now doing his or her own thing without the need of proclaiming it.

To put it another way: It is a question of balance between freedom and the experience of limitations, of being able to be fully myself and realizing that I am fully myself only in mutual dependence on others. Freedom is a paradoxical condition. A person in prison can be completely free in spirit. A person in utter destitution is not free if he has no options, no alternatives. I may have been so crippled emotionally by life experiences that I am unable to choose for myself, to exercise my freedom. I may be so totally self-centered that I believe that being free means being able to do whatever I please.

To put it concretely: This is the plight of young people, or anyone moving toward maturity. There is the need for the experience of freedom along with the experience of limitations and boundaries; the need for growth in personal decision along with a desperate need for strong guidance, honest models, loving controls.

Values cannot simply be imposed; there are too many conflicting systems. The weak norm that many fall back upon is: "Everybody is doing it." There are often conflicting values between husband and wife, between two different households on the same block, between teachers and professors, and peer groups, from whom young people receive contradictory messages.

We even have conflicting values in the Church. For example, the question of divorce, in which we ask which must be given priority: the institution of marriage, or the persons in the specific situation; or the controversial question of birth control.

Values must be discovered and freely chosen, internalized and appropriated, made our very own by personal acceptance and dedicated respect. Only then will they become the necessary foundation for personal decision and action.

But in this process of discovery and choice, we need to look beyond ourselves. We need to look for an ideal of justice and integrity. We need to discover our place and our role in a larger universe of being that finds its meaning in God.

God respects our freedom. He pleads and urges, he promises and threatens, too. But we must decide, we must face the consequences of our actions. God's mercy covers these consequences, as we see in the reading from Jeremiah where Yahweh pledges to save his people from exile.

In a time of conflicting values and lifestyles, we need to find the community, the culture, the system, the interpretation, the proclamation that seems to respond best to our needs, our understanding: the one that seems to make sense, to lead to a better world, to move us closer to the kingdom of justice and peace, brotherhood and equality, service and love.

We don't stand alone. We are responsible to each other even for our private lives, because our private lives are very much a part of what we are, and what we are is what we make available to one another. We are not our own norms, our own standards, our own judge.

Even Jesus received his call, his mission, his glory from the Father. We stand under the care and judgment of God as revealed in Jesus Christ. I firmly believe that his is a judgment of mercy, that when we are wrong we will be forgiven, but we as individuals stand under his judgment, we as a community stand under his judgment, and this judgment is expressed in many ways to us, even now.

If we don't stand alone, then if we wander and feel lost and need to find a home to which we might return, we have our parents and family, friends, community of faith and prayer, culture or subculture to which we can turn. If we make mistakes and find the burden of guilt heavy, we need to know where to find the word of forgiveness. If we discover that we are blind and cannot see where we are going, we must not be afraid to cry out to somebody else: Help me, that I may see.

May the Lord answer us with his healing touch, his noonday light, his forgiving blessing.

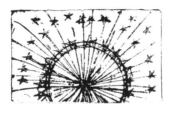

What Is Your Bottom Line?

TIME: NOVEMBER 3, 1991
SEASON: THIRTY-FIRST SUNDAY IN ORDINARY TIME
SCRIPTURE READINGS: DEUTERONOMY 6:2–6; HEBREWS 7:23–28;
    MARK 12:28B–34

Watching the news of the devastating fire in the Oakland hills this week, I asked myself: What would I take with me if I had to run away quickly from my house because of a fire? And then, when I was thinking about the homily, I asked myself: What would I want to take with me when I die? How wonderful it would be if, at the time of our dying, we could say that we had lived by the two great commandments to love God and neighbor!

Today, in both the first reading and the Gospel, we hear the Shema, the great affirmation of faith and love of God that the Jews pray every morning and evening, and at critical moments in life. Many a Jew walked into the gas chamber chanting: "Hear, O Israel! The Lord is our God, the Lord alone!"

That magnificent text has three different literary and historical settings in the book of Deuteronomy. The literary setting, the telling of the story, is on the banks of the river Jordan, between the wilderness and the land of God's promise, between homeless wandering and coming home. The people of Israel are on the verge of taking possession of the land. Moses, who will die before the crossing of the river, tells the people for the last time that they have only one God and that they should love him with all their being.

The historical setting for the writing of the book of Deuteronomy was toward the end of the period of the monarchy, when the people were prosperous and their affluence had left them complacent. They had sought and found security and well-being in their own strength and possessions, in sources other than the Lord of Israel, and they were at risk of losing everything.

The final edition of the book comes during the time of the Babylonian exile, and addresses people who have lost everything and are asking why. The message is about new possibilities, about returning to God in a new setting and with a new sense of identity. Now the book of the Law is the only possession they have, and it becomes the instruction for life.

Try to imagine how differently these words would be heard and spoken, treasured and prayed, in these three different settings: with eager expectation and gratitude as the centuries of waiting were about to end and the promises and hopes about to be fulfilled; with a certain amount of cynicism in the time of prosperity, when people felt that their success was the result of their own cleverness and hard work and they were proud of themselves and expecting God to be proud of them and favored by the fact that such a people would choose him as their God; and, having lost everything, with a new sense of humility, a new consciousness of their need for and dependence on God and his law.

No matter what the circumstances and the setting, the words have a ring of ultimacy, an unconditional character that even we cannot fail to hear. What is it that ultimately matters? I guess today we would ask: What is the bottom line? And the answer is: "The Lord your God you will love above all else, with all your heart and soul and mind!" What we ultimately value is constantly part of our life, always present to us, and the first thing we want to pass on to our children. That is why the verses that follow our reading say:

> Recite these words to your children and talk about them when you are at home and when you are away, when you lie down and when you rise. Bind them as a sign on your hand, fix them as an emblem on your forehead and on your gates. (Deut. 6:7–9)

The biblical injunction is clear and powerful: "The ultimate and abiding presence at the center of all of life is the Lord our God. The command is to live out of that ultimate truth."[51]

The gospel gives us one more setting for the Shema. The scribe, an expert in the Law, comes to Jesus to ask him: What is the bottom line? This question often occupied scribes and Pharisees in discussion as they studied the Law. There is no indication that the scribe had any ulterior motive in asking Jesus the question. He wanted to know his opinion, and there seems to have been a wonderful moment of understanding between them. They agree perfectly on the answer, and each affirms the other. The answer of Jesus is very much in the spirit of Deuteronomy, of the Law: "Love of God takes precedence over all other loyalties and desires, and when God's love engages the whole self, love of neighbor will follow."[52]

This connection between the love of God and the love of our sisters and brothers must have been very strong in the teaching of Jesus, because it is a major theme running through all the different writings of the Christian Scriptures. It is not possible to love God without loving one another. If we pretend that it can be done, we only deceive ourselves, because the God whom we say we love comes to us in the face and shape of our brothers and sisters.

What is the bottom line for us? What is of ultimate value in our life, in our thinking, in our acting, in the way we relate to one another and to the world? Spiritual writers have always urged that the best way to sort our priorities, the things that really matter, is to look at our life *sub specie eternitatis,* from the perspective of eternity, from the way things will appear when this life is over and we are about to enter the eternity of God.

Since the month of November is dominated by the memories and images of death and of the end of history and time, I thought we might ask the question of ultimate values in that context. If you can, imagine the moment when you become aware that you are about to die and ask yourself: What is the most precious treasure I am leaving my children, my family, my friends, my world? What is the fundamental value by which I have lived, that gives meaning to this earthly life of mine that is now coming to an end? What do you hope your answer will be?

It is even more important to ask: What is my answer now? It is here and now that we work out the final meaning of our life. I can only imagine what comfort, what peace, what trusting faith and sure hope would fill our hearts if we could say that we have tried our best to make God the ultimate value in our life, to love God first and foremost, with our whole mind and heart and strength, and to love others as we love ourselves in and out of this radical, ultimate, consuming love of God.

Through the Gospel Jesus proclaims to all of us today: "Listen, my people! The Lord our God is Lord alone! He alone is the Lord and meaning of your life! Love him with all your mind and heart and strength! And in his love, love yourself and love one another! There is nothing more important, nothing greater than this all-embracing love!" When you stop to think about it, this double-sided love is the only thing that we can take with us to the other side of death!

Giving Our All

TIME: NOVEMBER 6, 1994 (ST. GENEVIEVE, FRESNO)
SEASON: THIRTY-SECOND SUNDAY IN ORDINARY TIME
SCRIPTURE READINGS: 1 KINGS 17:10–16; HEBREWS 9:24–28;
     MARK 12:38–44

Can you think of a time when, like the widow of the Gospel, you gave not just from your surplus, but from the very substance of what you need for your life, from your livelihood, even ignoring your own needs? Have you ever given with that kind of generosity? I don't mean just giving money and material resources. I mean giving of ourselves, from all that we are and all that we have as persons, from all our gifts, our talents, our abilities. Have you given with that kind of abandon in your marriage, for example, or in friendship, at work, as parents, as members of a group for the greater needs of that community?

My own experience tells me that I always want to hold back a little, I always want to keep something for myself. It is very hard to give with that kind of generosity, and that is why the examples of the two widows, one in the first reading from the book of Kings, and the other in the Gospel, are so striking. Both of them give the very last little bit they have. The widow who gives to the prophet Elijah is preparing to die, and I wonder if that is not also the expectation of the widow of the gospel.

Try to imagine that Gospel scene. Jesus is in the temple, and he is watching the people coming and going. In the walls outside the women's court there were some trumpet-shaped containers into which people dropped their offerings. As Jesus is watching, the widow comes by and puts in less than a cent. Jesus calls the disciples over and says: "Look, look at that widow. She has given more than all the other wealthy people with all their fancy gifts."

In the context of the Gospel of Mark this passage is a powerful message of social justice. We find it in the middle of the controversies that Jesus is experiencing with the Pharisees, the scribes, the people in power. He has just rebuked them for building their power and wealth—even the grandiose temple—on the backs of the poor. He has just accused them of devouring "the houses of widows." And now he illustrates his point with the story of the widow giving her last penny. What a contrast! The irony is that her offering is going for the upkeep and beautification of the temple, which will soon be destroyed. At the time when the Gospel of Mark was being written, the temple either had just been destroyed or was about to be destroyed.

Jesus is praising the generosity of the widow, the powerless one, the one who has nothing. In a few minutes, when the gifts are brought to the altar here, remember that these are symbols of our own gifts, the gift we make of ourselves. Imagine Jesus standing here at the altar and watching what we are willing to give. What do we bring to the altar? How much are we willing to give of ourselves?

There will come a time in our life when we will not be able to hold anything back, the moment when we will come with all that we are and all that we have done to stand before the judgment of the Lord. That is the moment of our death. The month of November focuses our attention on the mystery of death. During this past week we celebrated the Feast of All Saints and the Commemoration of All Souls. Both celebrations invited us to remember all who have gone before us, to rejoice in their goodness and to offer our support in prayer for their continued growth in knowledge of the Lord and in intimate, loving union with God.

Your community here at St. Genevieve, the clergy and the whole Diocese of Fresno, have been touched by the death of your pastor, Fr. Francis Cheung. We all remember him as one who lived a life of service for others, who in many ways and at many times gave all that he had, did not hold anything back. I know he gave of himself to the end, through his suffering and his pain. I know he gave his death into the hands of the Lord for your sake and mine.

I hope that, when our time comes, all of us can do the same. But remember: We die as we have lived. If we want to be able to make that final gift of ourselves at the moment of death, we need to begin to look at the way we give of ourselves now. We need to prepare ourselves for the moment of death now, by growing in generosity, in the way we love God and one another, as the liturgy reminded us last Sunday.

We need to live in willingness to serve one another and to serve God's kingdom and God's people. We need to grow in detachment, letting go of the things that hold us back, the things to which we feel so attached that we can't be free. We need to grow in our trust and in our surrender to the living God so that we can give him truly all of ourselves when our death comes, knowing that we are safe in his hands, that he will care for us always.

That is the ideal way of looking at the mystery of death: to face it without fear, to prepare for it with a life of loving service, and to move toward it with complete trust and surrender to the God who loves us without limits and without conditions. Then we will be able to look ahead and to make our death the last act of self-giving, holding nothing back, giving all that we are.

One day that will happen. One day we will stand before God at the moment of our death, and at that moment we will be stripped of all our pretenses, all our façades, all the masks that we put on to make us look good and enable us to fool others—and perhaps even ourselves. But we need to begin the process of looking at ourselves and presenting ourselves honestly now.

Our church year is coming to an end. Next Sunday the liturgies will talk about the end of time and of history, the coming of the new heaven and the new earth. Two weeks from today we will celebrate the feast of Christ the King, the triumphal moment when everything will have been subjected to Christ and he will present everything to his Father, so that God will be all in all.

Today the liturgy calls us to do as the prophet Elijah did, to destroy all the false gods, all the false images in our life so that we can stand and face and worship the God of truth. The Word of God and the Eucharist we are about to celebrate have the power to transform us into vessels overflowing with God's grace and love, people filled with vitality and strength and worth, because of what God has done for us and in us. The more we are able to empty ourselves, the more the fullness of God will permeate our minds and our hearts and our whole being.

We make our own the Psalm prayer we prayed in response to the first reading: "Happy are we, whose help is the God of Jacob, whose hope is in the Lord our God. Because God keeps faith with us forever, he executes justice for the oppressed, and gives food to the hungry." The Lord will reign forever. Praised be the Lord.

Apocalypse Now?

TIME: NOVEMBER 17, 1985
SEASON: THIRTY-THIRD SUNDAY IN ORDINARY TIME
SCRIPTURE READINGS: DANIEL 12:1–3; HEBREWS 10:11–14, 18;
     MARK 13:24–32

On July 15, 1960, Jehovah's Witnesses gathered at the base of Mount Blanc, waiting for the end of the world. There are two reports of people who committed suicide at that time because they believed the world would come to an end and were afraid. Not too long ago, we read about a couple of families that had stopped all the activities of a normal life and locked themselves up in a house to wait for the imminent coming of the Lord. Following the same line when he explained why there was no need to worry about the conservation of resources, former Secretary of the Interior James Watt stated: "I do not know how many future generations we can count on before the Lord returns."

These are just some of the many examples of one way people interpret such passages from the Bible as we heard today, an interpretation best described as apocalyptic fundamentalism. Out of this perspective have come books such as Hal Lindsey's *The Late Great Planet Earth* and sermons from the likes of Oral Roberts, Jerry Falwell, and Herbert W. Armstrong.

The words *apocalypse* and *apocalyptic* come from a Greek verb that means "to lift a veil" in order to reveal hidden secrets. *Apocalyptic* is used to describe a literary style, a way of writing about the end of the world that speaks of visions and mysterious signs and cosmic conflict and cataclysmic destruction and the final victory of God and of God's chosen ones over the evil of the present time.

Contemporary apocalyptic fundamentalism interprets the Bible as a sort of coded book, containing the secrets of the cosmic battle and of the end of the world, hidden by God so that the elect, the saved ones at the end of time, could decipher them. For the apocalyptic fundamentalist, these passages describe literally, word for word, the history of our future, written in advance and accurate in every detail.

Although there are apocalyptic fundamentalists among Catholics, the teaching of the Catholic Church, especially in the documents of the Second Vatican Council, and the faith of great numbers of Christians of all denominations, interpret these passages very differently. Apocalyptic literature reflects the conditions of the time in which it was written. Because these were usually times in which the faithful believers were being persecuted, the writers used coded language to hide the meaning of their words from those in power over them. The message is one of hope: God will deliver his faithful ones, and good will triumph over evil. The writers describe the struggle and the victory in highly imaginary language and fantastic detail, because the reality is unknown and completely beyond the present experience.

What I am saying is not just theological abstraction. It has tremendous significance for the way we see life and the way we live. The apocalyptic fundamentalists fervently await nuclear war as the final cosmic battle marking the return of Christ and the end of the world. They are able to feel absolute confidence that they are among the saved. They expect Jesus to intervene miraculously to establish a thousand-year reign of happiness for the elect. They discount the effectiveness of all human efforts to build a new world. They know the signs of the end of time, and they recognize those signs in the current moral decline, political and economic chaos, the occupation of Jerusalem by Israel, communism as the evil empire, movements toward international unity such as the Common Market and the United Nations, and the ecumenical movement (especially the World Council of Churches). These are all manifestations of Antichrist and are to be resisted.

The Catholic interpretation of apocalyptic literature considers the battle described in the book of Revelation primarily as imagery. Catholic hope fervently seeks to avoid nuclear war and to preserve the earth. We have confidence in the power of God to save us, but we are reminded of our constant need to repent, to be forgiven and to forgive. We see Jesus at work in history now, working with and through human beings to build the kingdom of God on earth. We admit that we do not know the time of the coming of the Lord in glory or the shape of the world to come. We seek universal unity—religious, political, and cosmic—as the fulfillment of the plan of God.

These are not just differences of opinion but involve serious practical conflict. The Catholic stress on the Church, in its broadest meaning, as the sign and instrument of the unity of the human race and the clear call, for the sake of peace, for a worldwide public authority, are antithetical to the apocalyptic fundamentalist's view that a world church calling for international cooperation is the Antichrist. Catholic teaching, from the Second Vatican Council to the American Bishops' Peace Pastoral, sees the United Nations, even with its problems and weaknesses, as one of the few hopes for peace and international cooperation in facing the problems that threaten our world.

But the most significant and crucial difference is this: Our faith and our hope as Christians urge us to work and pray for peace and justice in the world. We are convinced that God is acting in the world to bring about universal reconciliation. The apocalyptic fundamentalists on the one hand seem to encourage conflict by branding other nations as "evil empires." On the other hand, they call for standing back and letting God do everything. In this way, they discourage efforts toward peace and a better world, even calling peace activists communists and the peace movement Antichrist. In the present critical time in human history, when destroying the world in a tragic parody of the Apocalypse is a practical possibility, we have reason to fear if many Americans share such attitudes.

We need not feel at a loss when we are confronted by apocalyptic preachers and their followers. We do hope for a new world, a new heaven and a new earth, and our hope is firmly placed in God and his saving power. We want to cooperate with God's loving, saving action for our world. Our belief derives from the Bible, from a full reading and careful study of the whole Bible, rather than a few apocalyptic texts. In our refusal to interpret the signs in an effort to determine the day and the hour of the end and transformation of our history, we are in good company. Jesus himself, in today's Gospel, tells us that no one knows that, not even he, but only the Father.

Christian hope urges us to live in the expectation of a new and better world, and to work for it and pray for it. I invite you to join me in doing both.

Love in Action

TIME: NOVEMBER 24, 1991

SEASON: CHRIST THE KING

SCRIPTURE READINGS: DANIEL 7:13–14; REVELATION 1:5–8;
JOHN 18:33B–37

The question Pilate asks Jesus is crucial for Pilate. He is looking for a reason to convict Jesus, searching for political grounds for his execution. When he asks: "Are you the king of the Jews?" he is really asking: "Are you a nationalist revolutionary, leading a revolt against Roman occupation?"

In the Synoptic Gospels—Mark, Matthew, and Luke— this question would have been heavy with irony. Especially in the Gospel of Mark, which we have been reading for this liturgical year that is coming to a close today, Jesus is always trying to correct the disciples' misunderstanding of his messianic role. They want him to be a messianic king, and he keeps telling them that he is a suffering servant. And when people come looking for Jesus to make him king, he runs away and hides in the hills. In the Synoptic Gospels we also find that brief moment of triumph when Jesus enters Jerusalem riding on the donkey, and people welcome him the way they welcomed kings, crying out: "Hosanna! Blessed is the one who comes in the name of the Lord! Blessed is the coming of the kingdom of our ancestor David! Hosanna in the highest heaven!" (Mark 11:9–10).

There is none of this in the Gospel of John. Out of the blue, Pilate asks Jesus if he is a king, and Jesus seems to accept the title, though the evangelist is careful to distance Jesus from the notion of royal messianism, by the assertion of Jesus that his kingdom is not of this world.

We must not misunderstand the phrase "not of this world" to mean some unearthly, immaterial, purely spiritual, heavenly reality. The "world" in which Jesus reigns is not some far off, unreal world. It is this world, the world into which he was born, into which he came "to testify to the truth" (John 18:37). But it is a different world, an alternate world that becomes Jesus' kingdom. It is a different vision that Jesus brings for this world, different from the model of control and fear, oppression and injustice, disregard for human dignity and rights, cruelty and violence, that was the world of Pontius Pilate and the Roman empire, and of the structures of society at the time of Jesus.

The world of Jesus is a world in which mutuality and sharing, respect and dialogue, invitation and empowerment define the relationships of those who belong to this world. In the Gospel of John, that is the way Jesus meets Nicodemus and the Samaritan woman, the blind man, and his friends Martha, Mary, and Lazarus. In the Gospel of John that is the way Jesus speaks to his disciples in that magnificent, moving, tender last conversation on the night before he was to die: "You are my friends. . . . I do not call you servants any longer. . . . I have called you friends, because I have made known to you everything that I have heard from the Father" (15:14–16). And what he has learned from the Father is that intimate communion of love that he wants to share with his friends. "As the Father has loved me, so I have loved you; abide in my love" (15:9); "Those who love me will keep my word, and my Father will love them, and we will come to them and make our home with them" (14:23).

We would be seriously mistaken if we were to understand this world as a totally private, personal world in which each one of us experiences this intimate, loving relationship with Jesus and the Father without any connection with one another. The same community of faith in Jesus that gave us the Gospel of John, also gave us the letters of John, with that incredible fourth chapter in the first letter in which we are told that the way we encounter God's love is in loving one another. "In this is love, not that we loved God but that he loved us and sent his Son to be the atoning sacrifice for our sins. Beloved, since God loved us so much, we also ought to love one another. No one has ever seen God; if we love one another, God lives in us, and his love is perfected in us" (4:10–12).

We are not called to some ethereal, mystical love of some ephemeral God whom we cannot see. We are called to love the God who continues to be incarnated in each of us, who lives in us, when we love one another. It is here that we find God's love, that we see God, in one another.

I never cease to be astonished when I stop to reflect on these words: "God lives in us and his love is perfected in us, when we love one another." It is not just human love, it is divine love that is at work in us. It is in this that we enter into the very mystery of God's own life. It is in this that we contribute to the growth—actually add to, increase, bring to perfection—God's own love: when we love one another.

I once mentioned the suggestion of a commentator that in the Gospel of John we should substitute "system" for "world." This makes it easier to understand that we are talking about our present reality, about different ways of experiencing, of living, this reality. We are not talking about love in some ideal world of feelings and sentiments. We are talking about this rough and tumble world. We are talking about love in action and deed, about being helpers and servants, as Jesus was.

Jesus, as Lord and Savior of the world, as king and ruler, presents us with the vision of a different system from the system of control and exploitation of those less powerful, of rivalry and competition to gain advantage over one another, of racism and social fragmentation to protect our privileges and the status quo. Jesus' world, Jesus' system, is one of mutual self-giving and loving inter-communion and mutually enriching interdependence.

To which system do we belong? To this world, or to Jesus' world? To the world's system or to the system Jesus came to initiate and embody in his own life and self-giving love? The reading from Revelation affirms with absolute clarity and conviction that: "Jesus Christ . . . the faithful witness, . . . has made us a royal nation of priests in the service of his God and Father" (1:5,6). You and I, all of us, were anointed with chrism in our baptism, as the ancient kings and priests were anointed, as Jesus was anointed by the Spirit.

We come today not only to celebrate the glory of Jesus our king, not only to affirm our hope in the final triumph of his kingdom when he returns in glory, but also to accept and renew our participation as active agents and actors in the work of preparing for his coming kingdom. We come to rejoice not only in the honor of being subjects of Christ the universal king, but also in the privilege of being priests in his royal nation, called with him and in him to service in love.

Jesus Christ is the faithful witness, the first-born from the dead and ruler of the kings of earth. To him who loves us and freed us from our sins by his blood, who has made us a royal nation of priests in the service of his God and Father—to him be glory and power forever and ever! Amen.

Notes

Notes

1. Milo Shannon-Thornberry, "Components of Lifestyle," *Living Simply: An Examination of Christian Lifestyles,* David Crean et al., eds., New York: Seabury Press, 1981, p. 11.

2. Ibid.

3. "Serving the Word," *Homily Service: An Ecumenical Resource for Sharing the Word,* Washington: The Liturgical Conference, 23:9 (Dec. 1990), p. 25.

4. See Jim Bitney and Yvette Nelson, *Living The Word Not Only on Sunday: Sunday Scriptures with Comments and Reflections,* Schiller Park, Ill.: J.S. Paluch Company, 5:5, Dec. 2–Dec. 30, 1990, p. 8.

5. Caryll Houselander, *The Reed of God,* p. 11.

6. David D. Thayer, S.S., *Homily Service,* 17:9, p. 44.

7. Raymond E. Brown, S.S., *The Birth of the Messiah: A Commentary on the Infancy Narratives in Matthew and Luke,* Garden City, N.Y.: Doubleday, 1977, p. 183.

8. Ibid., p. 199.

9. *Discalia II,* p. 59:103.

10. *Lumen Gentium,* #10. See 1 Peter 2:4–5, 9–10.

11. See John F. Hotchkin, "The Christian Priesthood: Episcopate, Presbyterate and People in the Light of Vatican II," *Lutherans and Catholics in Dialogue IV: Eucharist and Ministry,* Washington, D.C.: United States Catholic Conference, 1970, p. 203.

12. *Jerome Biblical Commentary,* 4:24.

13. "Studying the Lectionary," *Homily Service: An Ecumenical Resource for Sharing the Word,* Washington: The Liturgical Conference, 20:11 (Feb. 1988), p. 10.

14. Andrew Ciferni, *Homily Service,* 11:11, p. 31.

15. "Studying the Lectionary," *Homily Service: An Ecumenical Resource for Sharing the Word,* Washington: The Liturgical Conference, 20:11 (Feb. 1988), p. 36.

16. C. Hobart Mowrer, in Karl Meninger, *Whatever Became of Sin?* New York: Hawthorn Books, 1973, p. 195.

17. Father Joseph M. Champlin, *Together in Peace*.

18. See Richard N. Ostling, "Jesus Christ, Plain and Simple: A trinity of new, scholarly books tries to strip away traditional Gospel accounts of the man from Nazareth," *Time*, January 10, 1994, pp. 38–39.

19. Dominic Crossan, quoted in Ostling, op. cit., p. 38.

20. Tanya Luhrman, "Witches, magic, ordinary folks: Why entering a cult is comforting and feels a lot like joining a religion," *U.S. News & World Report*, April 7, 1997, p. 35. "Killing yourself for your religious beliefs is an extreme test of your faith. It is, thankfully, uncommon. On the other hand, it is the technique that carried the message of Christianity so powerfully in the early centuries of the first millenium. That Christians were will to martyr themselves rather than recant was a powerful testament to that faith. Those martyrs remind us that we can't take the easy route by saying that California cultists killed themselves because they were weirder than the rest of us." Luhrman is an associate professor of anthropology at University of California, San Diego, and author of *Persuasions of the Witch's Craft*.

21. "The Healing Word," *Homily Service: An Ecumenical Resource for Sharing the Word*, Washington: The Liturgical Conference, 27:1, p. 61.

22. Fr. Richard McCormick, S.J., writes about a growing consumer mentality toward children that soon might say: "Give me blue eyes this time." The consumer-item mentality toward children, combined with sophisticated prenatal diagnosis, will lead to an increasing emphasis on eugenics. Telling symptoms of the mentality are already apparent. We hear people refer to "the right to a healthy child." Implied in such loose talk is the right to discard the imperfect. What is meant, of course, is that couples have a claim to those reasonably available means to see that their children are as healthy as possible.

Barbara Katz Rothman has noted the erosion of the unconditional acceptance of the child implicit in "quality" thinking. She asks: "What does it do to motherhood, to women, and to men as fathers, too, when we make parental acceptance conditional, pending further testing? We ask the mother and her family to say in essence, 'These are my standards. If you meet these standards of acceptability, then you are mine and I will love you and accept you totally. After you pass this test.'

Barbara Katz Rothman, "The Products of Conception: The Social Context for Reproductive Choices," *Journal of Medical Ethics,* 11:4 (Dec. 1985), p. 190. Quoted in Richard A. McCormick, S.J., *Corrective Vision: Exploration in Moral Theology,* Kansas City, Mo.: Sheed and Ward, 1994, pp. 167-8.

23. "Ideas and Illustrations," *Homily Service: An Ecumenical Resource for Sharing the Word,* Washington: The Liturgical Conference, 27:2 (May 1994), p. 32.

24. Ibid.

25. Valerie Reddix, *Dragon Kite of the Autumn Moon,* New York: Lothrop, Lee & Sheppard, 1991.

26. C.S. Lewis, *Surprised by Joy: The Shape of My Early Life,* New York: Harcourt, Brace and World, 1955, p. 18.

27. "Studying the Lectionary," *Homily Service: An Ecumenical Resource for Sharing the Word,* Washington: The Liturgical Conference, 27:2 (May 1994), p. 52.

28. See Joseph G. Donders, *Praying and Preaching the Sunday Gospel,* Maryknoll, N.Y.: Orbis Books, 1988, p. 124.

29. *Good News,* New Berlin, Wisc.: Liturgical Publications, 18:6 (June 1991), p. 225.

30. "Studying the Lectionary," *Homily Service: An Ecumenical Resource for Sharing the Word,* Washington: The Liturgical Conference, 24:4 (July 1991), p. 13.

31. "Facing the Demonic, A Short Homily for July 14, 1991, 15th Sunday (B)," *Good News,* New Berlin, Wisc.: Liturgical Publications, 18:7 (July 1991), p. 262.

32. See Archbishop Weakland, "The Church's Crisis of Culture," *Origins,* 21:4, June 6, 1991, p. 68.

33. Reginald Fuller, *Preaching the New Lectionary: The Word of God for the Church Today,* Collegeville, Minn.: The Liturgical Press, 1974, p. 404.

34. Ibid.

35. Ibid., p. 405.

36. Joseph G. Donders, *Praying and Preaching the Sunday Gospel,* Maryknoll, N.Y.: Orbis Books, 1988, p. 132.

37. Found in *Time to Choose,* Lytchett Minster (Great Britian: Celebration, 1983), pp. 1131-114. Quoted in *Homily Service: An Ecumenical Resource for Sharing the Word,* Washington, D.C.: The Liturgical Conference, 22:5 (Aug. 1989), p. 10.

38. The Gospel of John is so focused on a single, specific approach to the spiritual life that I always feel the need of a corrective point, bringing out the fact that there is another dimension to the spiritual life, another approach to faith in Jesus Christ and love and union with God. As we read in Matthew: "Whatever you do to the least one of these you do it to me" (25:31–46). We do also encounter the Risen Christ in our brothers and sisters in need. We need both approaches to the mystery of God: the personal, spiritual, mystical approach to the Gospel of John, and the practical, compassionate approach of humble and faithful service to our brothers and sisters in need. the difficulty is in keeping a healthy balance between the two aspects of our spiritual life.

39. Raymond E. Brown, *The Gospel According to John I–XII,* Anchor Bible 29, Garden City, NY: Doubleday & Company, 1966, p. 292.

40. Ibid., p. 287.

41. Ibid., p. 284.

42. Ibid., p. 292.

43. "Studying the Lectionary," *Homily Service: An Ecumenical Resource for Sharing the Word,* Washington, D.C.: The Liturgical Conference, 24:5 (Aug. 1991), p. 40.

44. James A. Sanders, *Torah and Cannon,* Philadelphia: Fortress Press, 1972, p. 17.

45. Paul Dinter, "Preaching Commentary for August 1991 (B)," *Good News,* New Berlin, Wisc.: Liturgical Publications, 18:8, Aug. 1991, p. 292.

46. Richard McBrien, *Catholicism,* Minneapolis: Winston Press, 1980, p. 361.

47. Patrick J. Ryan, "The Only God: Twenty-fifth Sunday in Ordinary Time, September 22," *America,* 165:6, Sept. 14, 1991, p. 151.

48. In Harry James Cargas and Bernard Lee, eds., *Religious Experience and Process Theology,* New York: Paulist Press, 1976, p. 70.

49. *America,* 131:18, pp. 363–365.

50. Ibid., p. 362.

51. "Studying the Lectionary," *Homily Service: An Ecumenical Resource for Sharing the Word,* Washington, D.C.: The Liturgical Conference, 24:8, Nov. 1991, pp. 16-17.

52. Ibid., p. 18.

Index

D

S

Y